CONTENTS

Funeral Games
and
The Good and Faithful Servant

First presented by Rediffusion shortly before his death in 1967, *The Good and Faithful Servant* is a savage study of the disintegration of an old man when he retires after fifty sterile years in the service of a factory. More badgered than solaced by the attentions of the personnel officer and the works club for retired employees, George Buchanan's belated search for happiness lurches breathtakingly from moments of hilarity to moments of extreme pathos.

Funeral Games was first presented by Yorkshire Television in 1968. It is a play more outrageous, if possible, than *Loot* and as cracklingly witty. 'One imagines Orton, although dealing with bogus religion, a severed hand and a corpse in the cellar, had, like Wilde, only gaiety as a motive . . . Orton could turn the audience's gasp into a laugh, translating horror into humour, and leaving the viewers curiously aware of the simultaneous reaction. This is no mean talent and one could not help feeling sad last night knowing that this was the last of Orton's extraordinary wine.' Stanley Reynolds in *The Guardian*.

The photograph on the front of the cover shows Bill Fraser in the original production of Funeral Games, *and is reproduced by courtesy of Yorkshire Television: the photograph on the back of the cover is reproduced by courtesy of Douglas Jeffery.*

Printed in Great Britain by
Cox & Wyman Ltd., Fakenham, Norfolk

SBN 416 07380 8 Hard Cover
SBN 416 07390 5 Paperback

by the same author

ENTERTAINING MR SLOANE
LOOT
CRIMES OF PASSION
WHAT THE BUTLER SAW

METHUEN & CO LTD
11 NEW FETTER LANE · LONDON EC4

The Good and Fa

Introduction by Peter W

First published 19
Ltd © 19

INTRODUCTION

The Good and Faithful Servant may well come to be considered the best play Joe Orton wrote for television.

Funeral Games was a great tease, several lines have gone, I am afraid, into our family vocabulary – 'It's real. I can spot plastic fingers a mile off.' His brilliant and uniquely original ideas abound in this play. I must thank Yorkshire Television for allowing me to do it because there were quite a number of hazards – he used to put in the most devastating remarks, generally made by nuns, just to see me take them out.

The first television play I produced by Joe Orton was *The Erpingham Camp* which he had written either to tease me or because he genuinely believed that I was Cecil B. de Mille in his heyday at Paramount Pictures. He introduced a cast of hundreds and we had to set the Studio on fire. However, we did our best. I wonder if he was smiling guiltily when he dedicated *Erpingham Camp* and *Ruffian on the Stair* to me.

All the original plays written for television were uniquely directed by James Ormerod.

Joe was very puritanical; he did not smoke and drank very little; just to be social at parties.

He did not have a heart – but I loved what was there instead, which was infinite kindness and good manners.

He always put his fur boots on to escort me to the taxi rank.

His eyes were black as boot buttons.

We went to the Millais Exhibition at Burlington House. I bought the catalogue and we stared at some of the earlier paintings. They published in the catalogue the press comments of the day about the pictures: 'His notices were as bad as mine' said Joe.

Then we went on and had tea at Fortnum and Masons; he loved all the ladies' hats.

He telephoned every day either about his work or mine. His complete originality, which will be so evident in these two plays, is what I miss most of all.

PETER WILLES

Funeral Games

Funeral Games was first presented by Yorkshire Television on 25 August 1968 with the following cast:

PRINGLE	Michael Denison
TESSA	Vivien Merchant
CAULFIELD	Ian McShane
MCCORQUODALE	Bill Fraser
FIRST MAN	Richard McNeff

Director : James Ormerod
Executive Producer : Peter Willes

PART ONE

Scene One

Pringle's study.
CAULFIELD *enters.*

CAULFIELD. My name is Caulfield. We spoke over the telephone.
PRINGLE. I remember you distinctly. Do come in.

    CAULFIELD *closes the door.*

PRINGLE. Sit down. Or kneel if you'd prefer. I want you to behave naturally.

    Pause.

Shall I ring for a hassock?
CAULFIELD. These chairs look comfortable.

    He sits.

PRINGLE. They're unsuitable for trances. Are you a praying man?
CAULFIELD. I'm lost in thought occasionally.
PRINGLE. We've a house of contemplation, in the Arcade. Pay us a visit. (*Pause.*) Have you heard of my group? The Brotherhood. We hang about on street corners.
CAULFIELD. I've read of your activities in the Press. Weren't you had up for causing an affray?
PRINGLE. We were waylaid after conducting a 'God and You' meeting. Several of our members were arrested due to Jesuit intrigue. (*He takes a cigarette box from the desk.*) Have a herbal?
CAULFIELD. I'd rather smoke my own.

    He takes a packet of cigarettes from his pocket.

PRINGLE. Would you like to chew a bit of root I dug up in the garden of Gethsemane?
CAULFIELD. No. If it's all the same to you. (*He lights a cigarette.*)
PRINGLE. I never have to worry about dental decay since my Holy Land trip. (*Pause.*) Are you in need of refreshment?
CAULFIELD. I'm parched.

PRINGLE *takes a key from his pocket. He unlocks a desk drawer.*

PRINGLE. I've a bottle of water here from the Well at Bethsaida. (*He takes a stoppered flask from the cupboard.*) I have to keep it under lock and key. I can't trust the charwoman. (*He brings the flask to his desk.*) Will you have a nip?

CAULFIELD (*pause*). Is it pure?

PRINGLE. It's reputed to have miraculous powers. (*He pours some water into a glass.*) I use it as a laxative myself.

He puts the glass on the table beside CAULFIELD.

PRINGLE. What about food? Are you hungry?

CAULFIELD. Yes.

PRINGLE. Open the drawer at your elbow. You'll find a box of caraway seeds.

CAULFIELD *opens the drawer.*

PRINGLE. They represent many things to our sect. 'Food' being high on the list.

CAULFIELD *shakes a few seeds into the palm of his hand.*

PRINGLE. I'd like to ask you a question or two. Are you free from sin?

CAULFIELD. I'm as free as the next man.

PRINGLE. That's me. You're in good company. I could get into Heaven any time I chose. (*Pause.*) Have you ever had occasion to control yourself?

CAULFIELD. Yes.

PRINGLE. And succeeded?

CAULFIELD. Not since Christmas.

PRINGLE. Christmas. We call that the Festival of the Renewal of the Spirit. It's a time of rejoicing. We have a cot with a baby in it outside the church. I dare say you're surprised by the unusualness of the conception?

CAULFIELD. It sounds as though you have ideas of your own.

PRINGLE. We borrow from no one. Copies of my brochure *Blessings Abound* are still available. It'd be as well to purchase one. It gives the background to my teaching. (*Pause, he considers.*) What shape is your hot water bottle?

CAULFIELD. I haven't got one.

PRINGLE. Too proud. Mine takes the form of a cross. There's piety for you.

He stares hard at CAULFIELD.

CAULFIELD. Is there an ash-tray?

PRINGLE *picks one up. He brings it to* CAULFIELD.

PRINGLE. I stole this from under the very nose of a Doctor of Divinity. (*He puts it carefully beside* CAULFIELD.) I hope you never have occasion to do the same.

CAULFIELD *flicks ash into the tray.*

Are you available for hire? I've a job of work that wants doing.

CAULFIELD (*pause*). I won't be choirboy. I'm too old.

PRINGLE. We've no time for choristers in the Brotherhood. We've taken to handmaidens like ducks to water. We frown upon anything else.

He takes up a letter and hands it to CAULFIELD.

PRINGLE. Look at that.

CAULFIELD. What is it?

PRINGLE. An anonymous letter.

CAULFIELD. Who from?

PRINGLE. It's hard to say.

CAULFIELD. What does it accuse you of?

PRINGLE. Apart from a postscript suggesting that my lawn needs cutting, the writer is tolerant of my shortcomings. He brands my wife as an adulteress.

Long pause.

CAULFIELD *picks up the letter.*

CAULFIELD. It's a menu-type of hand. Have you insulted a café proprietor?

PRINGLE. I'm on bad terms with our tea-lady.

CAULFIELD. Have you seen her handwriting?

PRINGLE. I've never even seen her hands.

CAULFIELD. Get a glance at them. Maybe she isn't capable of committing the offence. (*He stubs out his cigarette.*) It gives the address where she misconducts herself.

PRINGLE. Hmm.

CAULFIELD. Where the intimacy takes place. Next door to a blue bookshop. I know the place well. It's run by a couple of ex-policemen.

PRINGLE. A love-nest adjacent to a bookshop. I do hope she hasn't betrayed me with a seedy intellectual.

CAULFIELD (*turning the letter over*). The watermark is in the form of a frog.

PRINGLE. A French intellectual would be even worse.

CAULFIELD. Is divorce against your code?

PRINGLE. We grant an annulment only in a case of possession by the Devil. If my wife is committing adultery my position would be intolerable. Being completely without sin myself I'd have to cast the first stone. And I'm dead against violence. I make no secret of my views.

   CAULFIELD *puts the letter away.*

CAULFIELD. I'll investigate this matter for you. Will I be paid?

PRINGLE. You'll receive a personal invitation to my exhibition of biblical documents. It's preceded by a buffet tea.

   They shake hands.

Make your report tomorrow. My candle burns until the third cock crow. (*He picks up some leaflets from his desk.*) Take these devotional reflections for your 'quiet time'. (*He opens the door.*) And should you wish to contribute to our Leprosy Mission you'll find a box in the hall.

   CAULFIELD *goes out.* PRINGLE *opens the door.*

Scene Two

MCCORQUODALE'S *room.*

TESSA. It's four o'clock. I've ordered my taxi. (*She places her hand on* MCCORQUODALE'S *brow.*) Has the attack passed?

MCCORQUODALE. Yes. I still feel fluttery. But I'll be all right.

TESSA. You were out for nearly an hour.

   She wipes his mouth with her handkerchief.

MCCORQUODALE. I heard you singing. I was miles away.

TESSA. It was a song in praise of sleep. The author took drugs and died of an overdose in Vienna at the turn of the century. (*She folds up the shawl.*) It's a pretty tune.

She puts the shawl aside and takes a cardigan from a drawer.

TESSA. I washed your face.

MCCORQUODALE. Whilst I was unconscious? You think of everything. (*He pinches her cheek.*) Did I wet myself?

TESSA. No.

MCCORQUODALE. That's because I'm wearing a device. I had it tailored by a young lady.

TESSA helps him to put on the cardigan.

TESSA. Did she see the wound in your thigh?

MCCORQUODALE. She made the sign of the cross.

TESSA. Was that helpful?

MCCORQUODALE. Another blister appeared shortly afterwards.

TESSA helps him.

TESSA. Why are you wearing a dog-collar?

MCCORQUODALE. Force of habit.

TESSA. It's illegal. You'll get into trouble.

MCCORQUODALE. It keeps me warm. Since I received my marching orders I've had stiff necks galore. (*He hobbles to the table, opens a drawer, searches.*) I had bad legs for years after I was forced to give up the Roman skirt.

TESSA. You were a Catholic priest?

MCCORQUODALE. I saw a vision of the Virgin once. She wore a floppy hat and had a sweet smile.

TESSA. You've mixed with the mighty, then? Did you ever meet the Pope?

MCCORQUODALE. Yes. I haven't seen him for years, though. He must be getting on now.

TESSA puts on her coat.

TESSA. How did you disgrace yourself?

MCCORQUODALE. I was outside the basilica of St Peter arm in arm with a couple of nuns. A mendicant monk objected to something I'd said. Made a terrible mess of my face with his crucifix. Oh, they're perfect fiends some of them.

TESSA *buttons up the coat. She picks up her hat, goes to the mirror.*

TESSA (*pause*). Who slashed the oil painting in the hall?

MCCORQUODALE. Someone from the public health.

TESSA *takes a lipstick from her handbag.*

MCCORQUODALE. Stay awhile. Another hour won't hurt.

TESSA. No. I must be off. I've business.

Pause.

MCCORQUODALE. You're still searching for your little friend?

TESSA. I found a man who saw her on a country road carrying a banner proclaiming the end of the world. But I don't think it has any significance.

MCCORQUODALE. I'll come with you tomorrow. We'll look in the park. She may be sleeping rough.

TESSA. There was nothing rough about Valerie.

MCCORQUODALE. We'll walk among the roses.

TESSA. Our names mustn't be linked. It would arouse comment.

MCCORQUODALE. You're hard, aren't you? I can't break down your resistance.

A taxi hoots from outside.

TESSA *looks from the window. She puts her lipstick into her handbag, closes the handbag, picks up a pair of gloves.*

TESSA (*pulling on her gloves*). I've laid out the needles. And the sterile wadding.

She kisses his forehead.

Tomorrow is library day.

MCCORQUODALE. Get me something with racy conversations.

TESSA. I'll phone you before lunch.

MCCORQUODALE. You're so exciting across the wires. You could be a terrible flirt if you'd only relax.

Taxi hoots again.

TESSA *picks up her handbag, goes to the door.*

TESSA. Nurse will be over in an hour to give you colonic irrigation. Hum to yourself if you're sad.

She goes out. Door slams. Silence.

MCCORQUODALE *reaches for his stick. He hobbles to the trolley.*

MCCORQUODALE. Oh, these contemporary young women. No romantic feelings. Brief and to the point. (*He picks up a hypodermic syringe.*) I must sort out my volumes of photographs. She might be interested in the visual arts. (*He rolls back his sleeve.*) My pictures of dizzy youth in pre-war Berlin. (*He fills the syringe from an ampoule.*) Those off-colour snaps of Frau Goebbels. (*He plunges the needle into his arm, gives a sigh.*) They'd make any man glad he wasn't a Semite.

He puts the hypodermic aside, picks up his stick, hobbles to the sofa. He turns.

CAULFIELD *is outside.*

CAULFIELD (*taking off his hat*). My name is Caulfield. I've broken into your house.

MCCORQUODALE. Did you force a window?

CAULFIELD. The wood was rotten. It gave way.

MCCORQUODALE. It's the worms. I sympathize with the timbers, having harboured the creatures myself.

CAULFIELD *twists his hat between his fingers.*

Come in. (*He returns from the door.*) Switch on the heater. My blood has ice in it. I'm like a penguin about the lumbar regions.

CAULFIELD *enters.*

MCCORQUODALE *sinks on to the sofa.*

CAULFIELD (*switching on the fire*). You shouldn't offer hospitality to rough young men. They might terrorize you.

MCCORQUODALE. It'd be something, wouldn't it? A step in the right direction. A bang on the nose is human contact. I've no money. My valuables amount to one slashed picture and an oleograph of an eighteenth-century lady. It was once spat upon by a maid of my mother's.

CAULFIELD *goes to the table. He picks up the hypodermic, examines boxes of pills, bottles of medicine.*

MCCORQUODALE (*pause, watching*). I've a dicky heart. So the possibility of murder mustn't be ruled out.

B

CAULFIELD. *puts the poker fireside companion set beside the boarded-up fireplace.*

CAULFIELD. I'm a sleuth. Employed by an irate husband. My cards are on the table.

MCCORQUODALE. I'm not a gambling man. I've seen the sorrow it brings.

CAULFIELD (*pause*). I'd like information about your companion. The little lady with the smile.

MCCORQUODALE. She's a health visitor.

CAULFIELD. Her husband is suspicious. He's a preacher of note. They sell the Bible on the strength of his name.

MCCORQUODALE. She never mentioned a husband. How remiss of her.

CAULFIELD. Adultery is a subject dear to his heart. He knows his onions.

MCCORQUODALE (*staring, aghast*). I haven't committed adultery. I wish to God I could.

CAULFIELD (*pause*). Are you past caring?

MCCORQUODALE. I'm past everything.

CAULFIELD. Have you tried nuts?

MCCORQUODALE. For a time. Indigestion was the only result.

CAULFIELD. Have you ever been birched?

MCCORQUODALE. By experts. I was being flogged for medicinal purposes before you were born. A Swedish gym instructress assured me that, with the correct treatment, I'd be glad to be alive at eighty.

CAULFIELD. What was the treatment?

MCCORQUODALE. Lettuce and sauna baths. Most disappointing.

CAULFIELD *chews his lip.*

CAULFIELD (*pause*). You swear no misconduct has occurred?

MCCORQUODALE. She's given me an enema once or twice. She did it with a sour face, though.

CAULFIELD *puts a cigarette into his mouth. He rolls it between his lips for a few seconds.*

CAULFIELD. How do you earn a living?

MCCORQUODALE. I'm a defrocked priest.

CAULFIELD. A holy man? Is there money in it?

He lights his cigarette with a taper from the pilot light on the electric fire.

MCCORQUODALE. Not any more. I bless a few babes in public parks to keep my hand in.

CAULFIELD *stubs out the taper into the sink. He turns to* MCCORQUODALE.

CAULFIELD. Speak to this woman again at your peril.

MCCORQUODALE. Is her husband up in arms?

CAULFIELD *nods.*

MCCORQUODALE. A jealous husband is no laughing matter.

CAULFIELD. You must give up seeing her.

MCCORQUODALE. That's hard. She's all I have. I'd hate to rely on nursie for company.

CAULFIELD. Isn't she no kind of fun?

MCCORQUODALE. She's a Welshwoman. Addicted to gambling. I go in fear of my life whenever she backs the wrong horse. Between the Derby and the Oaks I lost the skin from both buttocks. She was so careless. Woes nestle on my aged head like gathering swallows. I'm alone. Without faith. Staggering through a cruel and heartless world. (*He shakes with grief.*)

CAULFIELD (*pause*). Have you no family?

MCCORQUODALE. My wife is dead. A relief in many ways. I dreaded going first and having her leering round my death bed.

CAULFIELD. If you're lonely why not visit your wife's grave? You might meet people with similar interests.

MCCORQUODALE. My cellar is a God-forsaken spot.

CAULFIELD (*pause*). Is that where she's buried?

MCCORQUODALE. The actual burial was done by the National Coalboard. (*He faces* CAULFIELD, *earnest.*) She's under a ton of smokeless. I got it at the reduced summer rate.

CAULFIELD *stares. A sudden dawning. He gives a cry of horror and leaps away from* MCCORQUODALE.

CAULFIELD. You're a murderer?

MCCORQUODALE. These 'with it' expressions aren't familiar to me.

CAULFIELD. Wasn't it a happy marriage?

MCCORQUODALE. We bickered occasionally over the nature of God. Nothing more serious.

He takes a box of pills from his pocket.

CAULFIELD. Why did you kill her?

MCCORQUODALE (*swallowing some pills*). We belonged to a salvationist assembly: celebrating the Lord's Supper weekly and baptizing infants at the hinder end. One night I was watching and praying apart from the Brethren when I heard words which are not usual when saints meet. Upon investigation, I found our leader – a man known by the name of Bishop Goodheart – calling to order a number of female penitents on a straw mattress.

CAULFIELD. Was your wife with him?

MCCORQUODALE. She was. Standing in her true colours. And very little else. (*He gives a groan.*) Up to the Devil's tricks. And he was up to hers. Oh, the bacchic hound! And I'd given her my heart. (*He shakes, stricken by grief.*) My fury knew no bounds. I dragged her screaming into our caravanette which was parked in a lay-by. (*Pause.*) She was remarkably quiet on the way home. Later I discovered a broken neck, not a contrite heart, was responsible for her silence. (*Pause.*) I put her under the stairs until a heatwave – disastrous to the nation's water supply – almost undid me.

CAULFIELD (*pause*). What became of the Bishop?

MCCORQUODALE. He banished me for ever. Hurling curses as he ran.

CAULFIELD. Was 'Goodheart' his name in religion?

MCCORQUODALE. Yes.

CAULFIELD. What was his real name?

MCCORQUODALE. He didn't say.

CAULFIELD. Did that surprise you?

MCCORQUODALE. I've learned to accept the irrational in everyday life.

CAULFIELD *considers. He shrugs his shoulders.*

CAULFIELD. I'd get rid of the body. Take a tip from a member of the criminal classes.

MCCORQUODALE. All classes are criminal today. We live in an age of equality.

CAULFIELD. What are you doing to put yourself in the clear?

MCCORQUODALE. I go on my knees nightly.

CAULFIELD. Prayers won't keep the wolf from the door. (*Pause.*) Had your wife any relatives?

MCCORQUODALE. A father. He's blind.

CAULFIELD. Has he tried to contact you since your wife died?

MCCORQUODALE. No. He sent her a part share in a donkey for Christmas. So I'm in high hopes that he's going mad into the bargain.

CAULFIELD. Was she wealthy?

MCCORQUODALE. I can't touch her cheque book.

CAULFIELD. Why not?

MCCORQUODALE. My hand trembles so.

CAULFIELD (*pause*). Give me an example of her handwriting.
  He takes off his coat.
  MCCORQUODALE *opens a drawer in the table. He takes out a letter.*

MCCORQUODALE. This is an abusive letter she wrote to a Master of Foxhounds. It was returned wrapped around part of a dog-fox.
  He hands the letter to CAULFIELD *by the corner of the page.*
We neither of us finished our haddock that morning.
  CAULFIELD *puts the letter on the table. He shines a lamp on to the letter.*

CAULFIELD. Give me her cheque book.
  MCCORQUODALE *takes a cheque book from the drawer and gives it to* CAULFIELD.

MCCORQUODALE. Are you a forger?

CAULFIELD. I slept with one once.
  He writes a cheque with a flourish and hands it to MCCORQUO-DALE.

MCCORQUODALE (*after glancing at the cheque*). How refreshing to meet a genuine artist in today's world of highly praised fakes.

    CAULFIELD *puts on his coat.*

CAULFIELD. I've made it two hundred, to begin with. Can you manage the paying in?

MCCORQUODALE. Oh, yes. It's taking money out that causes the unpleasantness.

    CAULFIELD *picks up his hat.*

Don't go yet. I'm like a thing possessed at this time of the evening.

CAULFIELD. I've an appointment at the nude calendar shop. I've been commissioned to do February.

MCCORQUODALE. The *Church Gazette* put out a nice calendar. They might be able to use you. (*He hobbles to the sofa.*) Pass my shawl. I'm quite exhausted. I shan't sleep-walk tonight.

    CAULFIELD *wraps him in the shawl.*

MCCORQUODALE. How comfy I am. (*He pinches* CAULFIELD's *cheek.*) You're a good boy.

CAULFIELD. No. I'm bad.

MCCORQUODALE. As a bad boy you're a complete failure. Goodnight, lovey. Switch off the light.

    CAULFIELD *switches off the light.*

See me tomorrow. I welcome intelligent conversation at any hour of the day.

    CAULFIELD *goes out. Light falls from the window on to* MCCORQUODALE. *He breathes deeply, content.*

Scene Three

PRINGLE's *study.*
PRINGLE *at his desk. He is opening letters with a paper knife. He reads several. He puts them aside.*
CAULFIELD *enters.*
PRINGLE *wipes his mouth with a nervous gesture.*

PRINGLE. Is the prayer niche vacant?

CAULFIELD. Yes.

PRINGLE. I'll go down there in a bit. Knock up a few for the winning side. Did you speak to my wife?

CAULFIELD. No.

PRINGLE. Why not?

CAULFIELD. She refused to open the door. I heard bathwater running. She'd be naked, I expect.

PRINGLE (*sharply*). Did you imagine her without her clothes?

CAULFIELD. Yes.

PRINGLE (*pause*). I'd rather you didn't. It's no part of the bargain, is it? You were exceeding your duties. (*He returns to reading the letters.*) Make your report.

CAULFIELD. Your wife is engaged on a type of voluntary work. No more compromising than giving a blanket bath.

PRINGLE. Blanket baths are extremely compromising. Did you see her lover?

CAULFIELD. Yes.

PRINGLE. I've heard he lives like an animal. Is that true?

CAULFIELD. He's a defrocked priest. He made no secret of the fact that your wife was his only source of pleasure.

PRINGLE. What a disgraceful admission. He ought to be put in prison and visited by myself.

CAULFIELD. He hasn't infringed your marital rights. Your wife has done no wrong.

PRINGLE. It's too late now to say she's chaste. The fat is in the fire. (*He picks up a sheaf of letters.*) I had a remarkable experience last night. (*He puts the letters into a folder.*) The Lord came to me. I made a Covenant under the memorial arbour in the garden of the Lady of the Wand.

CAULFIELD. One of the Sisterhood?

PRINGLE. A woman of great humility and private fortune.

CAULFIELD. She's wealthy?

PRINGLE. She's a lost sheep with a golden fleece. We speak of her riches in hushed whispers. It means nothing to us.

CAULFIELD. Is she a philanthropist?

PRINGLE. She's a diamond. Lately she demonstrated her belief in Christian charity by building a synagogue on the banks of the Nile.

CAULFIELD. Is she Jewish?

PRINGLE. She's welcome anywhere. In Camden Town they call her Macushla. A very real honour. They accept that woman as a mother without question. In the garden of her detached ranch-type dwelling the vision of the Lord came upon me. I was swept up and the springs of my heart were opened. I made a vow. Taking my cue from Holy Writ. 'My wife must be punished.' The words I spoke weren't rejected or pooh-poohed. I was hoisted high on the shoulders of two priestly personalities. (*Tears roll down his cheeks.*) The Lady of the Wand shook out the glorious strands of her golden hair. There were loud hosannas. Palm branches. I was girt in white. The grounds of that Surrey mansion were ablaze with the ecumenical spirit until the small hours. My commandment was repeated like a catechism: 'Thou shalt not suffer an adultress to live.'

CAULFIELD (*pause*). You can't kill your wife. What about the sixth commandment?

PRINGLE. If she can break the seventh, I can break the sixth. Open that drawer. You'll find a gun.

CAULFIELD. What about the police?

PRINGLE. Christ didn't invite Pilate to the Last Supper. It would be as well to remember that.

He holds out his hand.

CAULFIELD. You can't shoot her. You're a member of the anti-blood-sports.

PRINGLE. That only applies to animals.

Pause.

CAULFIELD *opens the drawer. He takes out a gun.*

CAULFIELD (*handing* PRINGLE *the gun*). The civil arm will grasp the wrong end of the stick.

PRINGLE. No more argument. The humble and the meek are thirsting for blood.

He fires the gun and goes off.

Scene Four

MCCORQUODALE's *room.*

MCCORQUODALE *sitting in the armchair, a blanket over him.*

TESSA *enters with a large handbag. Pause. She puts the handbag down.*

TESSA (*pulling off her gloves*). Do you have anything to do with the old blind man who looks after the donkeys?

MCCORQUODALE. Is he a celibate?

TESSA. His donkeys are. It's part of their charter.

She takes off her coat and hangs it up.

Somebody put me on to him. He's supposed to be little Valerie's father. I found him in the yard. He was sending one of his charges away to be trained. Val was married he claims. (*Pause.*) Was your wife an amateur singer/accordionist?

MCCORQUODALE. She used to kick up a racket in her bath.

TESSA. This man says you married his only daughter.

MCCORQUODALE (*pause*). He's losing his wits. Donkey-minders are a byword for lunacy.

TESSA. What was your wife's name.

MCCORQUODALE. I called her Buzz.

TESSA. That was her pet name. You'd no right to be so familiar.

Silence. They face one another.

MCCORQUODALE *shivers. He stands abruptly to his feet.*

MCCORQUODALE. I must have a jab. My nerves are shot to pieces by your questions.

He hobbles to the table and rolls back his sleeve.

TESSA (*taking off her hat*). Where is she?

MCCORQUODALE *picks up the hypodermic syringe.*

What has happened to her?

MCCORQUODALE (*filling the syringe*). She packed her bags. Vanished into the night.

TESSA. Where to?

MCCORQUODALE. A nunnery. (*He injects the drug into his vein.*)

TESSA. I can find a list of recent vows taken in the trade paper of the monastic orders.

MCCORQUODALE. It's sold only to the pure in heart, and so, I'm afraid, has a limited circulation. You may have difficulty in obtaining a copy.

> *He hobbles back to the sofa.*

TESSA. I shall place an order with my bookseller. Why did she leave? Had you made life impossible?

MCCORQUODALE. Yes.

TESSA. You're a terrible tease. Have you always been like this?

MCCORQUODALE. I was even naughtier when I was young. The Unter Den Linden used to buzz with gossip as I passed by.

TESSA. The albums of photographs are most unsavoury. I'll say that to your face.

> *She opens her handbag and takes out a parcel.*

I've repaired the rent in your elastic bandage. (*She hands him the parcel.*) Go and get into the bath. I've brought my plastic apron.

> CAULFIELD *enters.*

CAULFIELD (*to* TESSA). May I speak to you? It's very urgent.

TESSA (*to* MCCORQUODALE). I shall give you post-sponge attention if we have time. Ring when you're ready.

> MCCORQUODALE *hobbles to the door.*
>
> TESSA *turns to her handbag.*
>
> MCCORQUODALE *exits.*
>
> TESSA *takes a plastic apron from her handbag.*

Who are you? And what do you want? I'm frightfully busy.

> *She shakes out the apron.*

CAULFIELD. Your husband is outside. He's going to murder you.

> TESSA *ties on the apron.*

TESSA. You must be mistaken. We celebrate our wooden wedding in a fortnight.

PRINGLE enters. He carries a gun. His face is pale.

PRINGLE (*to* TESSA). You've strayed from the paths of righteousness. I'm going to kill you.

TESSA. You'll be prosecuted. You haven't got a licence.

PRINGLE. Make your peace with God. On your knees. Pray, you sinner.

He advances, lifts the gun.

You'll soon be burning in some low, hot nook of Satan!

PRINGLE points the gun at TESSA's *heart. She backs away. Screams, suddenly afraid.*

CAULFIELD picks up a bottle and crashes it over PRINGLE's *head.*

PRINGLE drops the gun and falls to the ground.

TESSA (*pause, to* CAULFIELD). You want to be careful. You might hurt somebody.

CAULFIELD. Get a cold compress. Sponge his face.

TESSA goes out above table.

TESSA. Who put him up to this?

CAULFIELD. The Fathers of Love.

TESSA goes to the sink. She wets a towel.

Half his postbag this morning was from 'A Well-Wisher'.

TESSA. I know the name, but the face escapes me.

She returns with a towel. Kneels. Wipes PRINGLE's *forehead.*

PRINGLE revives.

He stares at TESSA.

PRINGLE. You're still alive? I've broken my vow. I'm unworthy of the name of Christian.

TESSA. What vow?

PRINGLE takes a newspaper from his pocket.

PRINGLE. The official organ has printed the text of my sermon with pictures and hostile comment. (*He opens the paper and shows it to* TESSA.) See the headline – (*Points.*) 'Pastor speaks his mind.' (*He lowers his finger.*) And underneath in heavy type: 'Sinners, stay away from Jesus.'

TESSA. Your words make powerful reading. (*She puts the paper aside.*)

PRINGLE. How shall I face the Lady of the Wand?

    PRINGLE *wrings his hands.*

PRINGLE. What shall I do now? To whom shall I turn?

    A bell rings.

CAULFIELD (*pause*). Perhaps we could pray.

PRINGLE. I'd be obliged if you'd treat this matter with due seriousness.

    The bell rings again.

CAULFIELD (*pause*). Why not forgive her?

PRINGLE. I won't tolerate forgiveness. It's a thing of the past.

CAULFIELD. Love thy neighbour.

PRINGLE. The man who said that was crucified by his.

    The bell rings.

    TESSA *goes to her handbag. She takes out a pair of rubber gloves.*

TESSA. Couldn't you just pretend to have murdered me? To save face?

PRINGLE. What an immoral suggestion.

TESSA. I could stay here with my elderly gentleman.

    She goes to the cupboard and takes out a tin of talcum powder.

CAULFIELD (*to* PRINGLE). You could say she'd gone to Australia. That's a synonym for death in the popular mind.

PRINGLE (*to* TESSA). She's shown no preference for the Colonies. Not even under hypnosis.

    TESSA *shakes powder into the rubber gloves.*

TESSA. During a mental disturbance at the age of fifteen I begged to be taken to Adelaide. My condition worsened after making the request.

    She puts the powder back into the cupboard.

CAULFIELD (*to* PRINGLE). Say she's on a surf-riding holiday. The quiet culture of the outback fascinates her. She takes up residence. And, after a decent interval, is swept out to sea on a rubber raft.

PRINGLE (*pause, to* TESSA). Would that suit you?

TESSA takes a scarf from her handbag and ties back her hair.

TESSA. It isn't the kind of death I'd hoped for. However, as long as I was fully dressed and had recently attended some place of worship I won't withhold my consent.

She rolls back her sleeves.

PRINGLE. The announcement can be made at my Blessing of the Spotless. I'll say you've made a journey to a far country. They'll think I've done you in and pray for your soul.

TESSA. Can I rely on that?

PRINGLE. Certainly. The Brethren are men of goodwill.

TESSA pulls on the rubber gloves.

TESSA. You'll find the manuscript of my history of our movement in the top drawer of my bureau. I'd like you to arrange publication to coincide with the news of my death. The photographs, taken by flashlight at our secret meetings, could be omitted if the publisher so desired.

PRINGLE. I'll see to it. Anything else?

TESSA. Remember never to smile again. It might arouse suspicion if you did.

PRINGLE. That'll be difficult. I've a naturally cheerful disposition. (*He kisses her cheek.*) You'll be sadly missed.

He picks up his hat and newspaper.

This'll be worth a million in publicity. Make a bit of a splash in the weekend Press. 'Vengeance is Mine', says 'No Nonsense Parson.' These human interest stories can increase a congregation a thousandfold.

He puts on his hat, opens the door, turns.

Trust in the Lord. We shall meet in the glory of the Infinite Morning. (*He nods and goes out.*)

The bell rings.

TESSA. I shall pretend to be Mr McCorquodale's wife. Valerie wouldn't mind. We've won prizes together.

CAULFIELD. Was she a personal friend?

TESSA. She kept her marriage dark. We'd lost touch to that extent.
Her father is a blind animal lover.

CAULFIELD. Is he mad?

TESSA. Yes, I think he is. It makes talking to him very difficult.

MCCORQUODALE enters wearing a ragged bathrobe.

MCCORQUODALE. I've been ringing and ringing. I'm out of my
rubbers.

TESSA. Where are your keys? I'm going to pose as your wife.

MCCORQUODALE. Oh, you dreadful up-to-the-minute people
with your unhealthy pranks.

*TESSA takes a bunch of keys from the pocket of MCCORQUO-
DALE's bathrobe.*

TESSA. Do these keys speak for themselves?

MCCORQUODALE. You're not to open doors without my permission.

TESSA puts the keys into the pocket of her apron.

TESSA. I'm going to make a tour of inspection. Follow me.

She goes out.

CAULFIELD (*to* MCCORQUODALE). You should've got rid of the
corpse. (*Pause.*) Did you cash the cheque?

*MCCORQUODALE hobbles to the sofa and lifts a cushion. He
hands several notes to CAULFIELD.*

CAULFIELD (*putting the money away*). I'll board up the cellar.

He takes off his jacket and goes out.

MCCORQUODALE hobbles to the table.

He picks up a pill box.

A bell rings.

MCCORQUODALE. Oh, my poor heart and kidneys are fluttering
like love-birds.

*He shakes pills into the palm of his hand and swallows them. A
bell rings.*

(*End of Part One.*)

PART TWO

Scene Five

PRINGLE's *study. Morning.*
PRINGLE *shaving with an electric razor.*
CAULFIELD *enters carrying a small parcel.*

PRINGLE (*over his shoulder*). Is that for me?

CAULFIELD. Delivered by hand.

PRINGLE. Open it. Was it a woman who brought it?
He switches off the razor and blows the hair from the blades.

CAULFIELD. She drove up in a Rolls. Gave the Commissionaire a quid. (*He unties the string on the parcel.*) You've had several mysterious women visitors lately.

PRINGLE. It's my unsavoury reputation. Attracts them like flies.
He puts the razor away and takes off his dressing-gown.
When rumour got around that I'd murdered my wife, my phone never stopped ringing. I had calls at every hour of the day and night. All from women making outrageous proposals.
He opens a leather case and takes out a brush and comb.
I've a different set of handmaidens for each of our ceremonies. (*He combs his hair.*) I'm ex-directory now.

CAULFIELD. I've read your book.

PRINGLE. *Hard Looks At God?*

CAULFIELD. It pulled no punches.

PRINGLE. They're filming *Tales of an Urban Hermit.* The proceeds will help to maintain and extend the ministry. (*He puts the brush aside.*) At the moment I'm caught up in politics. The wife of a top-ranking Russian diplomat came to me at the prayer centre and begged to be allowed to betray the Marxist cause.

CAULFIELD. You admitted her to your flock?

PRINGLE. I had no choice. She's heavy-breasted and sensuous. I didn't want to trigger off a third world war.

CAULFIELD has opened the parcel. He takes out a jewel box; opens it and removes a ring.

Ah! Is there a card?

CAULFIELD picks up a card.

CAULFIELD (*reading the card*). 'From a fervent admirer of Western Civilization.' (*He puts the card aside.*) Lenin would turn in his grave.

PRINGLE puts on the ring.

PRINGLE. I'm proud of the way she's accepted the life of the spirit. It hasn't been easy for her. She did two years in a forced labour camp for throwing caution to the winds at a swimming gala. You don't have to explain to her the advantages of living in a free society. Pass my jacket.

CAULFIELD hands him his coat and helps him into it.

Fifty guineas it cost the Russian people. New members are asked to indicate, by an immediate sacrificial gift, their partnership with the Brotherhood.

He opens a leather case and takes out a silver-backed clothes-brush.

This was a present from a woman journalist. She wanted the privilege of kissing hands that'd taken human life. It's so rare in her circle.

CAULFIELD takes the brush and takes a letter from his pocket.

CAULFIELD. This is for you. It was handed in early this morning.

PRINGLE. Open it.

CAULFIELD. It's confidential.

PRINGLE takes the letter. He opens it. He reads in silence.

PRINGLE (*putting the letter aside*). It's the product of a diseased mind. Public figures are subject to this kind of thing.

CAULFIELD picks up the letter.

CAULFIELD. Does it accuse you of murdering your wife?

PRINGLE. No. It says I didn't murder her. There's no end to the malice of people.

PRINGLE throws down the letter and CAULFIELD picks it up.

CAULFIELD (*reading the letter*). It claims your trendy success is a fraud. He's called Paterson. He's a crime reporter. He's calling on you for proof. (*He puts the letter down.*) Perhaps he's jealous of your success with women.

PRINGLE. The solution lies in his hands. He must murder his own wife.

CAULFIELD. Maybe he isn't married.

PRINGLE. Anyone can afford a licence.

He picks a Cologne bottle up from the desk, and pours Cologne on to his hands.

I shall seek professional advice.

CAULFIELD. Who from?

PRINGLE. My lawyers. It's a clear case of a private citizen being persecuted by the Press. It's defamation of character. I'll take them to court. (*He puts the stopper into the Cologne bottle.*)

CAULFIELD. For saying you're innocent? You'd never get away with it. There must be hundreds of innocent people in the country.

PRINGLE *picks up his watch and winds it.*

Pause.

You'll have to knuckle under. Provide him with evidence of your guilt.

PRINGLE (*putting on his watch*). A bloodstained sheet?

CAULFIELD. Where would you get the blood?

PRINGLE. One of our altar servers works in a blood bank. She'd know how to lay hands on a couple of pints.

CAULFIELD. You'd need a body.

PRINGLE. Are mortuaries in the Classified Trades Directory?

He turns to the telephone book.

CAULFIELD. A disappearing corpse would hit the headlines. They'd put two and two together.

PRINGLE (*pause*). What's to be done? Think of the scandal. I'd never live it down if I were found innocent.

CAULFIELD (*pause*). You don't need a complete body. An arm would do. (*Pause.*) Or a head.

c

PRINGLE. Where could I get a human head? Even Harrods wouldn't accept the order.

CAULFIELD. Is there anywhere I could get a meat cleaver?

Long pause.

PRINGLE. I'm part owner of the Pixies' Den. Try the kitchen after two o'clock. (*Pause.*) You won't strike down any member of the staff, will you? They're impossible to replace.

CAULFIELD. I'll respect private property.

He picks up his hat.

I shall take a stroll in London's country. Commune with nature.

PRINGLE. You're not going head-hunting in Epping Forest?

CAULFIELD. I shall look in on your late wife and her saintly lover. You can arrange a meeting with the gentlemen of the Press.

PRINGLE. You'll provide evidence of murder?

CAULFIELD. Where can I contact you this afternoon?

PRINGLE. At the Russian Embassy. I'm cementing East-West relations till four.

CAULFIELD. I'll give you a ring.

He turns at the door.

Be seeing you.

He goes out.

PRINGLE *picks up the letter. He glances at it and goes to the telephone.*

Scene Six

MCCORQUODALE's *room.*
Neater. A flowered cloth on the table. A bowl of fruit centre.
MCCORQUODALE *reading a newspaper, a rug over his knees.*
TESSA *enters with a shopping bag, carrying a sheaf of circulars. She puts down the shopping and glances through the circulars.*
TESSA. They're having a sale of damaged carpets. (*She throws the*

circulars into the wastebin.) The fires do get at these firms, don't they?

She takes the shopping from the bag.

I heard noises from the cellar. Is it open?

MCCORQUODALE (*without looking up*). Young Caulfield is down there. (*He folds his newspaper.*) Your husband is in the news again.

TESSA. Is he?

MCCORQUODALE. Questions are being asked about your murder.

TESSA. I never think about it now.

MCCORQUODALE. You were upset at first though, weren't you?

TESSA. Well, nobody likes to be done in. It stands to reason.

MCCORQUODALE. He's made a lot of enemies. The Convocation of Canterbury are in a huff. They'll come for him one of these days.

> TESSA *puts the shopping away. She folds up the shopping bag and puts it into a drawer.*

TESSA. They came for little Valerie's father last night.

> MCCORQUODALE *takes off his reading glasses and puts them into a case.*

MCCORQUODALE. Recent figures show that the mad will out-number the sane by the turn of the century.

TESSA. They never publish any comforting statistics, do they? These computers are always out to frighten people.

> CAULFIELD *enters wearing jeans and a singlet vest. His hands and face are smeared with coaldust. He carries a meat cleaver and a human hand, severed above the wrist, wrapped in sacking.*

TESSA (*to* MCCORQUODALE). I've bought a cake.

MCCORQUODALE. Is it an anniversary?

TESSA. No. It's a Dundee.

> *She takes a cakestand from the cupboard and puts a doily upon it.*

> CAULFIELD *puts the meat cleaver aside.*

CAULFIELD (*to* MCCORQUODALE). I couldn't get her head off. It must be glued on.

MCCORQUODALE. She was always a headstrong woman.

CAULFIELD. I had to take a hand instead.

TESSA (*to* CAULFIELD, *over her shoulder*). Do you want to wash your hands before tea?

CAULFIELD. Yes.

> TESSA *picks up a teapot and goes out.*
>
> CAULFIELD *goes to the sink. He washes the hand and his own.*

MCCORQUODALE. How was she looking?

CAULFIELD. Black. And very uncomely.

MCCORQUODALE. She'll be mistaken for coloured in Heaven.

CAULFIELD. Do they let them in there?

MCCORQUODALE. One hears conflicting reports.

> CAULFIELD *dries his hands.*

CAULFIELD. Is there a box to carry it away in?

> MCCORQUODALE *rises and searches. He picks up the cake tin and hands it to* CAULFIELD.

MCCORQUODALE. Use that. Give it back when you've finished.

> CAULFIELD *puts the hand into the cake tin and puts the lid on the tin.*
>
> TESSA *enters with the teapot. The kettle boils.*
>
> CAULFIELD *goes to the table. He puts the cake tin beside his chair.*
>
> TESSA *pours water into the teapot.*

CAULFIELD (*to* MCCORQUODALE). D'you want this?

MCCORQUODALE. Her watch?

CAULFIELD. It came off once the wrist was severed. No proper support, see.

> TESSA *brings the teapot to the table and cuts the cake.*

TESSA (*to* CAULFIELD). They're looking for a bright youngster to represent Britain. You ought to go in for it.

> *She puts a piece of cake on to a plate and hands it to* MCCORQUODALE. *She does the same to* CAULFIELD.

The young woman by the bridge has left her husband.

> CAULFIELD *puts the watch on.*

Rows over a snake. (*She pours tea.*) She was looking forward to a rabbit or a guinea-pig. Something for baby to play with. (*She hands a cup of tea to* MCCORQUODALE.) Then he tells her he's put a deposit on a five-feet-long python. (*She hands tea to* CAULFIELD.) She was horrified.

She sits, picks up her own tea.

Isn't it wicked, though, allowing a snake to jeopardize your marriage?

> CAULFIELD *reaches for the sugar bowl.*

> TESSA *hands it to him.*

Is that a new watch?

CAULFIELD. Yes. (*He puts sugar into his tea.*)

TESSA. It's a lady's. (*She drinks.*)

CAULFIELD. Yes.

TESSA. You want to be careful. People are funny about that sort of thing.

> CAULFIELD *puts the sugar bowl aside. Pause.*

Let me see.

> CAULFIELD *hesitates. He holds out his arm.*

TESSA (*pause*). Take it off. Give me a look.

> CAULFIELD *takes off the watch. He hands it to her. She examines it.*

TESSA (*pause*). This is little Val's watch!

MCCORQUODALE. It's a well-known make. Could be anybody's. (*He dips his cake into his tea.*)

TESSA. No. She had everything individually styled. See! (*She shows* MCCORQUODALE *the back of the watch.*) Her personal emblem – a ballet girl blowing a kiss. She had it on all her belongings. (*To* CAULFIELD.) Where did you get this?

CAULFIELD. I found it. In the street.

TESSA. This has decided me. Something terrible has happened. (*She opens her handbag, and puts the watch into it.*) I shall take my troubles to the Police.

CAULFIELD. Haven't they got enough of their own?

TESSA. Val had a lot of friends in the Police. She used to sing songs in praise of Authority at her concerts.

She puts the cake on to a tray and clears the table. She puts the cups and saucers on to the tray.

She may be a prisoner. I was once touched on a tube train. Women aren't safe today. They should bring back the harem. We've got to be protected.

She puts the tray on the sideboard and looks about her, puzzled. She comes back to the table. Pause. She sees the cake tin and stoops to pick it up.

CAULFIELD. No! I want that tin!

TESSA (*indignant*). So do I. The cake will go stale. (*She takes the tin to the kitchen.*)

    MCCORQUODALE *and* CAULFIELD *exchange glances.*

    MCCORQUODALE *takes a box of pills from his pocket, shakes two into the palm of his hand and swallows them.*

    TESSA *wraps the cake in a piece of foil.*

    CAULFIELD *approaches the sink.*

CAULFIELD. Don't open that tin.

TESSA. Why not?

CAULFIELD. I bought a plastic hand from a Novelty shop. I put it into your cake tin.

    TESSA *turns from wrapping up the cake.*

TESSA. That was very silly of you. Neville down the road is in trouble of that sort. His little playmate had a convulsion. Her mother is putting it into the papers. (*She lifts the tin.*) I'm glad you had the sense to tell me.

    She takes off the lid and looks in. She gives a shriek of horror.

(*Gasping with fright.*) It's real.

MCCORQUODALE. Plastic.

TESSA. It's real. (*Trembling.*) I can spot plastic fingers a mile off.

    She turns to the sink and pours glass of water. She drinks.

A human hand in a Dundee cake tin. Whose is it? Do we know?

MCCORQUODALE. He found it in the long grass.

CAULFIELD. It'd been left by a courting couple.

MCCORQUODALE. It answers to the name of 'Billy'.

TESSA *puts the glass down.*

TESSA. Was the watch with it? (*Pause.*) I'm seeing the Sergeant at Val's station.

She reaches for her coat.

MCCORQUODALE. I won't have you going to the Police. I've criminal tendencies.

CAULFIELD. He's been using the alias Leonard Field to obtain preferential treatment at a West End store.

MCCORQUODALE. I've a roomful of stolen footwear downstairs.

TESSA. Is that why I'm never allowed into the cellar?

MCCORQUODALE *turns. He picks up a bottle of smelling salts and holds them under his nose.*

What has happened to your wife?

MCCORQUODALE. She was taken up to Heaven. In a fiery chariot. Driven by an angel.

TESSA. What nonsense. Valerie would never accept a lift from a stranger. (*She turns to the door.*) I'm going down to gauge the full extent of your crimes.

She goes out.

MCCORQUODALE (*pause, weary*). In the closet you'll find a rope.

CAULFIELD *opens the cupboard.*

I bought it a month ago. I intended hanging myself.

CAULFIELD. What stopped you?

MCCORQUODALE. The weather turned nice.

CAULFIELD *takes the rope from the cupboard.*

MCCORQUODALE. Tess is a member of the Book of the Month club. Sound in wind and limb. You'll have to manage on your own. (*He hobbles round the chair.*) I'm much too frail.

Screams from below.

CAULFIELD *runs the rope through his fingers.*

The door bursts open. TESSA *enters. Tears in her eyes.*

TESSA. Oh, poor little Valerie. Who did that to her? (*She sobs.*)

CAULFIELD *loops the rope into a noose and slips it around* TESSA's *throat from behind. He drags her choking to the floor.*

Scene Seven

PRINGLE's *study. Night.*
PRINGLE *chanting.*

CAULFIELD. Did you have your interview, with the Press?

PRINGLE. With the Press?

CAULFIELD. You established your guilt?

   PRINGLE *closes the bible.*

PRINGLE. He was an atheist. He took one look into that cake tin and fainted. These people without religion are broken reeds.

   He stands, walks to the mirror, straightens his tie.

When he came to, he kept asking how I could face God with a murder on my conscience. Which is ridiculous coming from a man who doesn't believe in God.

CAULFIELD. And anyway you haven't done a murder.

PRINGLE. Precisely. It takes no effort at all to face someone who doesn't exist with a murder that hasn't happened.

CAULFIELD. Did he go quietly?

PRINGLE. I got one of the Fathers of Love to throw him out. (*He puts on his coat.*)

CAULFIELD (*pause*). I'm having trouble with your wife. You ought to know how things are.

PRINGLE. I'll send a bunch of flowers by special courier.

CAULFIELD. I don't know how we're going to keep her quiet.

   PRINGLE *swings round, faces* CAULFIELD, *startled.*

PRINGLE. It wasn't her hand?

CAULFIELD. No. (*Pause.*) McCorquodale murdered his wife. It was her hand.

PRINGLE. She can have it back. It's not on permanent loan.

CAULFIELD. She was Valerie Fenton before her decease.

PRINGLE. Has my wife seen the body?

CAULFIELD. Yes.

PRINGLE. What happened?

CAULFIELD. She seemed genuinely upset.

PRINGLE. Well, Valerie was an old school-friend. They were very attached. She used to attend our meetings. Her salvation was assured.

> CAULFIELD *opens a drawer in the desk and takes out the gun. He holds it out to* PRINGLE. PRINGLE *shrinks away.*

What are you asking me to do?

CAULFIELD. Kill your wife.

PRINGLE. I've already killed her once. I couldn't do it again. I'd be a murderer.

CAULFIELD. You are a murderer. In the eyes of the world. I'm only asking you to live up to your public image.

PRINGLE. That's a terrible thing to ask a man to do.

CAULFIELD (*pause*). Unless you kill your wife she'll accuse you of not being her murderer.

> *He takes* PRINGLE *by the arm and shoves the gun into his pocket.*

You're a clergyman. It's time you practised what you preach.

> *He leads* PRINGLE *to the door.* PRINGLE *stops. He turns round.*

PRINGLE. We mustn't forget the hand.

> CAULFIELD *goes back to the desk. Picks up the cake tin. He returns to* PRINGLE.

We've a short-sighted tea lady. I don't want her handing that around in the mid-afternoon break.

> *They go out.*

Scene Eight

MCCORQUODALE's *room.*
TESSA *bound hand and foot, strapped to a chair.*
MCCORQUODALE *enters, dragging a large cabin trunk.*

TESSA. Untie me.

MCCORQUODALE. You'd escape.

TESSA. I'll forget what I've seen.

MCCORQUODALE. A mutilated corpse isn't something that'd slip my memory. But you young people are heartless. The whole post-war generation.

TESSA. Set me free.

MCCORQUODALE. I'm your gaoler. I can't possibly aid your escape. This isn't a State prison, you know.

He drags the trunk to the centre of the room and sits, exhausted by the effort.

Oh, I'll never survive a second murder. There's so much work involved.

He picks up his inhaler and inhales deeply. He tries to force back the catch on the trunk.

I'll ring nursie tomorrow. I need one of her medical romps.

He tugs at the catch unsuccessfully.

TESSA (*pause*). Let me help you. My feet are bound. I shan't run away.

MCCORQUODALE (*stands, picks up a pair of scissors*). It's most irregular. This is to be your coffin. It's tantamount to the undertaker employing the corpse.

He cuts the bonds on TESSA's *wrists.*

TESSA (*kneeling*). What a lovely old trunk. Is it antique?

MCCORQUODALE *puts the scissors out of reach.*

MCCORQUODALE. It was purchased from a man who sailed to the Far East in search of adventure. He died of a skin complaint in Rangoon.

TESSA *forces back the clasp.*

It's full of souvenirs of happier days. My childhood was idyllic. I had the run of a Convent until I was eight. And then the Reverend Mother decided, quite wisely, that I was a threat to the chastity of her flock.

TESSA *pushes back the lid.*

So I was turfed out. The first of life's many bitter disappointments. I'd already decided, you see, to take the veil.

He kneels beside TESSA. *He lifts a book from the trunk.*

A history of the Ursulines written by an ex-member of the

Order. This was smuggled into the Convent and read against
Mother's wishes. It contains many errors of doctrine.

He wipes dust from the book and puts it aside.

*TESSA takes several objects from the trunk, dolls, a stuffed bird,
a bundle of letters, a Cardinal's biretta. She lifts out a small
framed painting and holds it up.*

TESSA. A watercolour.

MCCORQUODALE. It was my intention to represent – in a sym-
bolic fashion – the Christian Church.

TESSA. A bird of prey carrying an olive branch. You've put the
matter in a nutshell.

MCCORQUODALE *wipes a tear from his eye.*

MCCORQUODALE. These mementoes of a blameless life contrast
sadly with my present predicament. (*He weeps.*)

TESSA. Why did you kill poor Val?

MCCORQUODALE. All my misfortunes stem from a self-styled
bishop. That wretched lackey in the Almighty's house has
brought my grey hairs in sorrow to the grave.

He sobs, uncontrollably.

*TESSA picks up a dagger from the bottom of the trunk and cuts
through her bonds. She stands to her feet.*

Pause.

You're free?

TESSA. I found a dagger at the bottom of the trunk.

MCCORQUODALE (*standing, reaching out*). My knife for circum-
cising the Faithful.

TESSA. You've been a Muslim, too?

MCCORQUODALE. Well, in Algiers during the depression. I had
to live. Don't betray me.

He staggers towards her, a hand to his heart.

TESSA. Truth must win. Otherwise life is impossible.

She turns to the door and opens it.

PRINGLE and CAULFIELD are outside.

They enter, pushing TESSA aside.

CAULFIELD stands by the door.

PRINGLE (*to* CAULFIELD). Who is that man?

CAULFIELD. Your wife's lover.

MCCORQUODALE (*to* TESSA). Who is this man?

TESSA. My husband.

PRINGLE (*to* CAULFIELD). His name in God is Brother Sinceritas. He badly injured me whilst I was engaged in a holy act.

MCCORQUODALE (*to* TESSA). This is my arch-enemy. I endured humiliation at his hands in the greenwood. This is Bishop Goodheart. Take my dying curse. You diabolic crumb from the table of the damned!

    He slaps PRINGLE *across the face.*

PRINGLE. I'll teach you to strike a man of admitted charity.

    He seizes MCCORQUODALE *by the throat and shakes him.*
    MCCORQUODALE *gasps with fury. He attempts to escape. They fall about, buffeting one another.*

CAULFIELD (*pause*). What an amazing sight – two men of God trying to throttle one another.

    MCCORQUODALE *breaks free. He staggers to the table, wheezing and spluttering.*

MCCORQUODALE. You ecclesiastical poltroon. You won't escape your just deserts. I'll see every soul in Christendom knows that the blood on your hands is a fraud.

    He holds his inhaler to his mouth and takes deep gulps.

PRINGLE. You have no proof.

    MCCORQUODALE *puts the inhaler aside. He pulls* TESSA *to him.*

MCCORQUODALE. Here's my proof. I'll produce your wife like a rabbit from a Shakespearian hat.

    Pause. PRINGLE *picks up the knife from the floor.*

PRINGLE. I'll have you yet. You anti-Christian pimp and witches' comfort.

MCCORQUODALE. Being a man of goodwill I'm well prepared for violence.

    He transforms his stick into a dagger and prods PRINGLE *to a distance.*

TESSA. You mustn't cause trouble. I shall deny that I'm alive.

MCCORQUODALE. I'll kill you, then.

He grabs her, and holds the sword to her breast.

TESSA. You can't destroy me. I'm the evidence.

PRINGLE. You can't expose his guilt without establishing my innocence.

CAULFIELD *takes the gun from* PRINGLE's *coat and fires.*

TESSA, PRINGLE *and* MCCORQUODALE *scatter. Pause.*

TESSA (*running behind sofa*). Who's he after?

PRINGLE. You.

CAULFIELD *fires again.* PRINGLE *disappears.*

TESSA *throws the meat cleaver at* CAULFIELD. *It crashes among the medicine bottles, and drops down beside* MCCORQUODALE.

MCCORQUODALE. Oh, be careful. My pills.

Pills rain down upon him from the upset boxes. He crouches under the table.

CAULFIELD *approaches the screen and pulls it away.*

TESSA *is trapped. She shrinks away.*

TESSA. No. Don't touch me. Please, let me alone.

CAULFIELD *pushes the gun into her face. He pulls the trigger. Click of barrel turning. He pulls the trigger again. Click of barrel turning.* CAULFIELD *examines the gun.*

CAULFIELD. It's empty.

TESSA *gives a cry of relief and bursts into tears.*

TESSA. Somebody is going to pay for Val's death.

MCCORQUODALE (*crawling from under the table*). Oh, my Lord Bishop, you should never have taken on that extra female penitent.

PRINGLE. You should've kept your evil temper under control.

MCCORQUODALE. You were teaching her tricks not even a grandmother should know.

TESSA. Was he misbehaving with Val?

MCCORQUODALE. He was making a breach in the seventh commandment and my wife. (*To* PRINGLE.) That's foul churching, Bishop.

TESSA (*to* PRINGLE). How long had it been going on?

PRINGLE. The spirit of the Brotherhood entered Valerie about a year prior to her death.

TESSA. How could she sink so low?

CAULFIELD. He got in under her guard. It's a familiar technique of dance-hall seducers.

TESSA. She was so well brought up.

CAULFIELD. It's the well brought up ones that go first. As every small-time Romeo knows.

TESSA. Stealing my husband and concealing the fact that she had one of her own. It's scandalous behaviour.

> PRINGLE *picks up* TESSA's *coat. He holds it out for her.*

PRINGLE. This will have to come out at the trial?

TESSA. What trial? She tempted the Lord. It would be blasphemous to raise a hand in her defence. (*She buttons her coat.*)

> *The three* MEN *exchange looks.*
>
> TESSA *goes to the mirror. She puts on her hat.*

PRINGLE. None of this must leak out. You realize that, don't you? The Brethren would be ruined.

MCCORQUODALE. What about the corpse?

CAULFIELD. I'll take it to a deserted warehouse. (*To* PRINGLE.) You can identify her as your wife. Recognize her from some familiar article of jewellery.

TESSA (*turning from the mirror*). Take my badge from the Legion of Believers.

> *She unpins the badge from her coat and hands it to* CAULFIELD. (*To* PRINGLE.) What will happen to me?

PRINGLE. You'll remain as the wife of Bishop Bonnyface. (*To* MCCORQUODALE.) I'll confirm the appointment later.

TESSA (*to* MCCORQUODALE). Shall I be your wife in name only?

MCCORQUODALE. Unless a miracle occurs.

CAULFIELD. I must have transport for the body.

PRINGLE. You can't use my van. It has 'God' printed on it.

TESSA. Use our portable chapel. It has a detachable altar.

CAULFIELD. I'll have to be compensated.

PRINGLE. In what way?

CAULFIELD. Taken on to God's payroll.

PRINGLE. We use volunteer labour in the vineyard of the Lord.

CAULFIELD. Have you ever been blackmailed?

PRINGLE. You'd be well advised not to try your tricks here. We're Children of Light. Not criminals. Tangle with the Prince of Peace and you'll find a knife in your back.

MCCORQUODALE. That's quite true. I myself once threw holy water in a woman's face. Marred her for life.

CAULFIELD. I was merely demonstrating the vulnerability of your position.

PRINGLE. I'll arrange for you to be shown the priestly path. You're a photographer's model?

CAULFIELD. Yes.

PRINGLE. I'm publishing my life story in picture form. I might use you to illustrate 'Glad Tidings'. (*To* MCCORQUODALE.) Was your wife given a Christian burial?

MCCORQUODALE. No.

PRINGLE. We must repair the omission.

    CAULFIELD *picks up the cake tin.*

CAULFIELD. We've the hand here. Can't we take the rest of her as read?

PRINGLE. Yes. That would be in order. (*He takes the tin.*) Pass me a book – and a bell.

    TESSA *goes to the bookcase.*

    CAULFIELD *opens the cake tin. He looks in. He takes out a human hand.*

    TESSA *draws a horrified breath.*

    MCCORQUODALE *flinches.*

    CAULFIELD *lifts out the hand. He breaks off a finger with a sharp crack.*

CAULFIELD. This isn't a real hand. It's a fake.

    PRINGLE *hurries across. He examines the hand.*

PRINGLE. Paterson. He's deceived me. Oh, the malice of the heathen is terrifying.

MCCORQUODALE. What would he want with a human hand?

TESSA. He might use it as a paperweight.

CAULFIELD (*to* PRINGLE). He's got evidence. We're sunk.

Knocking on the door.

The door opens. Two MEN *enter.*

FIRST MAN. We are plain-clothed Police Officers. We've a warrant to search these premises. (*Shows warrant.*) Who can identify the remains of the woman in the cellar?

PRINGLE. She was my wife.

FIRST MAN. Did you kill her?

PRINGLE. She was an adulteress.

FIRST MAN. You'd better come along with us. (*To his* COMPANION.) Book the others as accessories.

MCCORQUODALE. Shame. Shame. It'll be banner headlines. The daughters of the Philistines will rejoice.

PRINGLE. Let us go to prison. Some angel will release us from our place of confinement.

The door is opened.

Do not weep. Everything works out in accordance with the divine Will.

The POLICE *lead them out.*

The Good and Faithful Servant

'Well done, thou good and faithful servant.'
Matthew. 25 : 21

'Faith, n. Reliance, trust, *in*; belief founded on
authority.'

Concise Oxford Dictionary

The Good and Faithful Servant was first produced on television
by Rediffusion on 6 April 1967 with the following cast:

BUCHANAN	Donald Pleasance
EDITH	Hermione Baddeley
MRS VEALFOY	Patricia Routledge
DEBBIE	Sheila White
RAY	Richard O'Callaghan
AN OLD MAN	Jack Bligh

Director : James Ormerod

Scene One

A long corridor.
Closed doors left and right line the corridor. From behind them come sounds of typing. A telephone is heard ringing, faintly.
At the end of the corridor, EDITH, *an old woman, is scrubbing the floor.*
BUCHANAN, *an old man, wearing a commissionaire's uniform, makes his way along the corridor towards* EDITH. *He stops beside her. Out of breath.*

BUCHANAN. Is this the Personnel section?

EDITH. Yes.

BUCHANAN. I've found it at last. I've had a long journey.

EDITH. Didn't they provide a map?

BUCHANAN. No. I was offered a guide, but I turned it down.

EDITH. Are you expected?

BUCHANAN. Yes. I'm retiring today. They're making a presentation. I'm the oldest living employee. My photograph will be in the firm's magazine. They've already arranged the particulars. I gave them every assistance, of course.

    EDITH *wrings water from a cloth into a bucket.*

I recall them building this block. My first day here coincided with the Foundation ceremony.

    EDITH *looks up.*

EDITH. So did mine. I was crushed up against a wall by a section of the crowd. My mother complained on my behalf. But nothing official ever came of it.

BUCHANAN. How long have you worked here?

EDITH. Fifty years. I have breaks, of course. For pregnancy and the occasional death of a near relative.

BUCHANAN. I've been here for fifty years, too. How strange we've never met.

EDITH. Which gate do you use?

BUCHANAN. Number eight.

EDITH. Ah, well, you see, that explains it. I've always entered by number fifteen.

She moves her bucket and cloth down the corridor.

BUCHANAN. I've a feeling we have met. In the distance, as I came along, there seemed something familiar. Something about your stance. Something that awaked memories.

EDITH begins to scrub the floor.

You've a look about you of the only woman I ever loved. I was a youngster when I met her. She was in difficulties by the roadside. I hesitated long enough to let her know I was a gentleman, and then I spoke. I attended to her problem and she was grateful. She let me see her home. And as luck would have it, our way lay through a meadow and the grass was high.

EDITH stops, looks up, gives a startled cry.

I'm sorry if I've offended you. These highly spiced tales aren't for the ears of the elderly. I apologize.

EDITH. No! Go on! What happened?

BUCHANAN. I couldn't tell you. I'm too ashamed. And she's been dead for years, I suppose. I can't bring disgrace upon her name.

EDITH. What was her name?

BUCHANAN. I can't recall. Though it was dear to me once.

EDITH. Was it Edith Anderson?

BUCHANAN. Yes. It was. How did you know?

EDITH stands. Tears glisten in her eyes.

EDITH. It was me!

BUCHANAN (*recoils*). You!

EDITH tugs off her plastic glove and shows him her hand.

EDITH. You gave me this ring.

BUCHANAN stares at the ring. Pause. Stares into EDITH's face.

BUCHANAN. But . . . (*He shakes his head.*) . . . you were so beautiful.

EDITH. I remained desirable until I was thirty.

BUCHANAN. You lasted so long?

EDITH. Then I had my first illness.

She puts on her glove, kneels, painfully, begins to scrub the floor.
You did me a great wrong.

BUCHANAN. No one knew.

EDITH. Not at the time. Later on it became only too obvious that I'd gone astray. I was turned out by my father. I wandered for a long time until I found somewhere to have the babies.

BUCHANAN. Two?

EDITH. Twins.

BUCHANAN. Promiscuity always leads to unwanted children, I should've known. Where are they now?

EDITH. In Heaven, I hope.

BUCHANAN. Dead?

EDITH. Killed in Italy.

BUCHANAN. What were they doing so far from home?

EDITH. They were wounded in a skirmish and taken to a peasant's hut for shelter. The peasant's son offered them water from a poisoned well – he meant no harm – it was an accident. The sanitary system of an alien country killed them. The authorities were good. They chose to believe that it was war wounds. I've the papers at home.

BUCHANAN takes out a handkerchief, blows his nose, bows his head.

BUCHANAN. Is there nothing left of them? No photographs?

EDITH. Before they died, they produced a son.

BUCHANAN. With whose help?

EDITH. A young girl of impeccable character who worked in a pub.

BUCHANAN. Was it legal?

EDITH. No.

BUCHANAN. Which one fathered the child?

EDITH. No one knows.

BUCHANAN. Their morals must surely have been below average?

EDITH. It was the conditions. You couldn't blame them. We were so frightened in those days. You lived through it same as I did. They panicked, I expect.

BUCHANAN. Is our grandson alive?

EDITH. Yes. I look after him. When he's settled I shall die.

BUCHANAN. What of?

EDITH. Does it matter?

She moves the bucket farther down the corridor, kneels again, painfully.

BUCHANAN. You have philosophy then? (EDITH *nods, begins to scrub the floor.*) Are you resigned to anything in particular?

EDITH. No. Life in general. Isn't that enough?

BUCHANAN *stands beside a door marked 'Mrs Vealfoy'.*

BUCHANAN. Shall I see you again?

EDITH. That would be pleasant.

BUCHANAN. Are you married?

EDITH. I was.

BUCHANAN. What became of your husband?

EDITH. He ran away during the depression.

BUCHANAN. I'll look you up. Expect me tonight.

He knocks on the door.

MRS VEALFOY (*calls*). Come in.

He opens the door.

Scene Two

MRS VEALFOY'*s office.*

MRS VEALFOY *sitting at her desk. She looks up, smiles.*

MRS VEALFOY. Do come in.

BUCHANAN *enters.* MRS VEALFOY *indicates a seat in front of the desk.*

BUCHANAN *sits.*

MRS VEALFOY. May we be completely informal and call you 'George'?

BUCHANAN. By all means.

MRS VEALFOY. Good, good. (*Laughs.*) My name is Mrs Vealfoy. I expect you know that, don't you?

BUCHANAN. I've seen you at functions organized by the firm. You're usually in the distance. I've never been close before.

MRS VEALFOY. That's right. I remember you well. (*Laughs.*) I have to ask you one or two questions.

She passes a printed form across the desk.

Fill that in, George.

BUCHANAN *begins to fill in the form.*

Are you excited?

BUCHANAN. Yes.

MRS VEALFOY. That's good, isn't it? (*Laughs.*) Your overalls, boots, gloves and any other equipment or clothing belonging to the firm must be given up by three-thirty. Ask your foreman or head of department for details.

BUCHANAN *hands back the form.* MRS VEALFOY *initials it and puts it into a wire tray.*

Have you your clock card with you?

BUCHANAN *hands her his clock card. She initials it and puts it into the tray.*

Are you a member of a union? Are your dues paid?

BUCHANAN. In full.

MRS VEALFOY. You leave the firm with no unpaid debts, no arrears of credit?

BUCHANAN. Yes.

MRS VEALFOY. Have you in your possession any object belonging to the firm? Any machine part, tools, plans of the premises? I'm sure you realize we can't be too careful.

BUCHANAN. I've nothing you'd want.

MRS VEALFOY. You're not free to divulge any information about the firm, the administration of the firm, or the firm's products. We should take proceedings, you see. (*Pause.*) You lost a limb in the service of the firm? (*She consults a file on her desk.*) You conceal your disabilities well.

BUCHANAN. I had therapy treatment in the medical wing of the firm's Benevolent Home.

MRS VEALFOY. And the pension paid to you by the firm for the loss of your arm plus the cash was legally binding. We are in no way responsible for your other limbs. If they deteriorate in any way the firm cannot be held responsible. You understand this?

BUCHANAN. Yes.

MRS VEALFOY hands him his National Insurance card.

MRS VEALFOY. Your 'cards', George.

They both laugh.

I think that's everything. Did we take your photograph?

BUCHANAN. Yes. (*Pause.*) Something was said about taking another – as I was leaving the firm. But I don't want any fuss made.

MRS VEALFOY. We have no intention of taking any more photographs. So you won't be bothered.

BUCHANAN (*with a laugh*). It's no bother to me.

MRS VEALFOY. It's no bother for you, I'm sure. (*Laughs.*) But we mustn't put upon you.

She takes her hat from the hatstand and puts it on.

BUCHANAN (*pause*). You aren't putting upon me. Whatever gave you that idea? Let them take as many photos as they like.

MRS VEALFOY (*at the mirror*). You hold the record for long service? Is that correct?

BUCHANAN. Quite correct. I'm hoping my grandson will come here. To carry on the tradition.

MRS VEALFOY turns from the mirror. She goes to the desk. She consults the file. She stares at BUCHANAN sharply.

MRS VEALFOY. Pay attention to me! What grandson? You've no descendants living. I have the information from our records.

BUCHANAN. I've just learned of a descendant of whom I had no knowledge.

MRS VEALFOY. Who told you?

BUCHANAN. A woman I met in the corridor.

MRS VEALFOY. Had she any right to inform you of an addition to your family?

BUCHANAN. She was the boy's grandmother.

MRS VEALFOY. Your wife is dead! Have you been feeding false information into our computers?

BUCHANAN. The woman wasn't my wife. I was young and foolish. It happened a long time ago.

MRS VEALFOY. I shall inform your section manager. He must straighten this out with Records.

BUCHANAN. It's a personal matter. My private life is involved.

MRS VEALFOY. Should your private life be involved, we shall be the first to inform you of the fact.

She opens the door.

Let my secretary have your grandson's address. I'll send him some of our literature.

Scene Three

The works canteen.

On a table at the end of the room are two parcels. Several MEN *and* WOMEN *are sitting in front of the table.*

BUCHANAN *and* MRS VEALFOY *enter. Applause.* MRS VEALFOY *holds up her hand for silence. She smiles.*

MRS VEALFOY. We all know why we are here. George Buchanan is retiring today after fifty years with the firm. Now, I want to tell you a little bit about him.

She smiles and looks at BUCHANAN. *Applause from the crowd.* George left school at fourteen and joined the firm one year later, receiving the princely sum of seven shillings a week – which he will tell you went a long way in those far-off times. He quickly became known for his speed and intolerance of any work which was in the least 'slip-shod'.

She looks around her and at BUCHANAN. At the outbreak of the Second World War, George was called upon to supervise his department, and to take on a lot of extra responsibilities. He didn't complain, though. He shouldered his share of the burden which we all had in those days.

She pauses. She looks around the room. Her voice takes on a quieter, more meaningful note.

George has had his share of life's tragedies. We all remember reading that he was on the danger list some years ago. He soon returned to us, however, and his cheery laugh echoed once again through the canteen. He is now fit and still rides a bicycle. Nothing could quell George, I'm sure.

Friendly laughter.

I think, looking at him, we can hardly believe he will be sixty-five on Sunday. He is looking forward, I know, to an active retirement. And it is with retirement in mind that the men of your department, George, have pleasure in presenting you with this very lovely electric toaster. Which I believe, is what you wanted.

She unwraps the first parcel and hands the toaster to BUCHANAN. *Applause.*

And, as a parting present from the firm, I have great delight in giving you this electric clock.

She unwraps the second parcel and hands the clock to BUCHANAN. *Applause.*

When you look at it, you'll think of us, I'm sure.

Applause. BUCHANAN *clears his throat. Silence.*

BUCHANAN. As I stand on the eve of a well-earned rest I have no hesitation in saying that I've worked hard for it. (*Pause.*) Over the years I've witnessed changes both inside and outside the firm. The most remarkable is the complete overhaul of equipment which has taken place during the last year. I am truly sorry to leave without seeing much of it in operation. But – there it is – what will be, will be.

Pause.
He nods his head.

As I say, retirement is a big step. It's going to mean a break.

But I can say I've earned my rest. I hope to see you at the annual 'get together' in a month's time. So it isn't by any means 'Goodbye'.

MRS VEALFOY looks at the clock. It is twelve-thirty.

Well, I had better come to an end now, as I think the canteen ladies are impatient to begin serving dinner. So once again, thank you. God bless. And – thank you – thank you.

Cheers. The clatter of dishes. The clock says just after twelve-thirty. The AUDIENCE *push past* BUCHANAN *and* MRS VEALFOY. BUCHANAN *and* MRS VEALFOY *are alone beside the table.*

MRS VEALFOY. Make sure you hand in your uniform. After lunch you're free. We've no further need of you.

She smiles, and goes out. BUCHANAN *is alone. He picks up the parcels, joins the lunch queue. No one speaks to him, or is aware of his presence. The queue moves forward.*

Scene Four

MRS VEALFOY'*s office.*

MRS VEALFOY *at her desk. A knock on the door.* DEBBIE *enters.*

DEBBIE. Are you the lady that gives personal hints as well as for the firm?

MRS VEALFOY (*with a bright smile*). My advice covers all fields of endeavour. Won't you come in?

She indicates a seat. DEBBIE *closes the door and enters the room.*

MRS VEALFOY. What is your department?

She turns to the filing cabinet.

DEBBIE. I'm a typist. I've recently been transferred from the pool to the special services section. I'm highly recommended.

MRS VEALFOY *speaks from the filing cabinet.*

MRS VEALFOY. What is your name?

DEBBIE. Debbie Fieldman. (*Pause, with a nervous cough.*) I'm filed under Deborah.

MRS VEALFOY *takes a file from the cabinet and sits at her desk.*
She smiles at DEBBIE.

MRS VEALFOY. How can I help you?

DEBBIE. I was more or less bludgeoned into coming to you by a
friend of mine. You may recall helping her out of a sticky spot
when she was up before the council about the rateable value of
her flat?

MRS VEALFOY. Yes. I remember the girl well.

DEBBIE. She left the firm under a cloud, but she certainly profited
by your advice. (*Pause, she bites her lip.*) I don't know where to
begin. I'm nearly at my wit's end.

MRS VEALFOY. Take your time. Speak slowly and distinctly.
I'll be listening to every word.

DEBBIE *twists her fingers together. Her lip trembles.*

DEBBIE. Well, you see, Mrs Vealfoy, I've become intimately
attached to a boy who means all the world to me. Against my
better judgement, I allowed him to persuade me to do something which I knew to be wrong. Oh, you'll never know what
I've been through these last few weeks . . . (*She blows her nose on
her handkerchief.*)

MRS VEALFOY (*quietly and with compassion*). Are you having a
baby, my dear?

DEBBIE. Yes.

MRS VEALFOY. Have you seen a doctor?

DEBBIE. Yes. I went to the hospital and said I was married. I had
to make up many of the details. I regret having to deceive the
Health Service in this way, but I daren't go to our doctor. My
secret wouldn't be safe for a second with him. We're on the
telephone at home, you see. And the doctor is always ringing us
up at inconvenient hours, and coming round . . . so I went to the
Out Patients. (*She bursts into tears.*)

MRS VEALFOY *comes round the desk and puts an arm round*
DEBBIE's *shoulder.*

MRS VEALFOY. Is the young man willing to marry you?

DEBBIE. I haven't asked.

MRS VEALFOY. You must.

DEBBIE. I can't.

MRS VEALFOY. Why not?

DEBBIE. I hardly know him.

MRS VEALFOY. Well, you must get to know him. Try to win his confidence. Has he any hobbies to which he is particularly attached?

DEBBIE. No.

MRS VEALFOY. Where does he work?

DEBBIE. He's unemployed.

MRS VEALFOY. Where did you meet him?

DEBBIE. He's never asked me to meet him. I usually do it by accident.

  MRS VEALFOY *shakes her head: the unusualness of the case has her baffled for a moment.*

MRS VEALFOY. This is a shocking state of affairs. Do you know the young man's name?

DEBBIE. He asked me to call him Ray. What his motive was in asking me to do such a thing, I can't say. I was half asleep at the time. I'm not trying to excuse his behaviour. Or mine. I've always taken it for granted that he knew what he was up to.

MRS VEALFOY. He's got you into trouble, and he may have done it under an assumed name. That fact has to be faced. (*Pause.*) Have you told your parents yet?

DEBBIE. No.

MRS VEALFOY. Would they object to your having a baby?

DEBBIE. Mum would die. She couldn't put it in the paper, see. She'd feel she'd been cheated.

MRS VEALFOY. What about your father?

DEBBIE. He's always had a horror of anything unnatural. It'll come as a blow to him. He's only just got over the shock of my brother.

MRS VEALFOY. You'd better say nothing for the moment. You must arrange a definite time and place of meeting with the young man. Pin him down. Get him to come clean over the matter of his name. That is most important. And then contact me.

She scribbles a note and hands it to DEBBIE.

That is my telephone number.

DEBBIE *puts the note into her handbag.* MRS VEALFOY *glances at her watch. She opens the desk and takes out a brochure. She hands it to* DEBBIE.

MRS VEALFOY. Here is a plan of the firm's nurseries. You may wish to book a place for the child now. I can do it for you.

DEBBIE. But I'm not married.

MRS VEALFOY. You will be, my dear. Leave everything to me.

MRS VEALFOY *smiles.* DEBBIE *puts the brochure into her handbag.*

Scene Five

The firm's clothing store.

A curtained cubicle, outside the cubicle, a tailor's dummy dressed in the trousers, shirt, tie, shoes and hat belonging to BUCHANAN'S *uniform.*

A MAN *in a brown overall takes the uniform coat which* BUCHANAN *hands through the curtains. He puts it on to the dummy. Wheels it slowly away.*

BUCHANAN *enters from behind the curtains, dressed in his own clothes. He appears smaller, shrunken and insignificant.*

He watches the MAN *in the brown overall pull a dust sheet over the tailor's dummy.*

BUCHANAN *shuffles from the store.*

Scene Six

EDITH'S *living-room.*

She enters, followed by BUCHANAN. *He is carrying two parcels. He places them on the table.* EDITH *stares in amazement.*

EDITH. Oh!

BUCHANAN. What is it?

EDITH. Your arms! Where has the extra one come from?

BUCHANAN. It's false.

EDITH. Thank God for that. I like to know where I stand in relation to the number of limbs a man has.

She opens the first parcel.

An electric clock. (*She lifts it from the wrapping.*) They gave you the wire as well. Shows how much they think of you.

She opens the second parcel.

A toaster. It's a good make too. We must have toast for tea to try it out.

She puts the parcels to one side and looks at BUCHANAN *fondly.*

What a day. You'll re-live it many times in the future.

BUCHANAN *takes the toaster, begins to strip the wires, attaches plug to flex.*

EDITH. I've several souvenirs of our children dotted about this room. I'll point them out later. When you've settled in. (*Pause.*) This tablecloth belonged to the mother of our grandson. She left it me in her will.

BUCHANAN. Is she dead?

EDITH. She took her own life, poor dear. When the boys were killed. She couldn't face the idea of living on, so she gassed herself. She was illegitimate as well. That was the bond between them.

BUCHANAN. Is there no respect for marriage in this district?

EDITH. Very little, you'll find.

BUCHANAN *pauses in his work. Looks up.*

BUCHANAN. What are we going to tell Raymond?

EDITH. Do we have to say anything?

BUCHANAN. Oh, yes. It wouldn't be fair to keep it a secret.

EDITH. It will be a shock to him to learn that the older generation behaved in such a disgraceful way.

BUCHANAN. We must explain the circumstances. Ask him to be tolerant. We are going to get married after all.

EDITH (*pause*). Isn't it too late?

BUCHANAN. It's never too late for marriage. I'm surprised at you, I am. Talking like the worst elements in Society. We must put things to right. We'll do it quietly and without fuss.

Door slams.

EDITH. This is Ray. He always makes a noise when he enters. It's a tradition with him.

RAY *enters.* EDITH *smooths her dress and smiles.*

EDITH. Ray, I want you to meet someone. Mr George Buchanan.

RAY *shakes hands with* BUCHANAN.

RAY. Good evening.

BUCHANAN. I'm pleased to meet you, Raymond. Your grandmother has said a lot in your favour.

He sits. EDITH *looks at* BUCHANAN. *Looks at* RAY, *a worried frown on her face.*

EDITH. Sit down, Ray. I've something to say to you which may come as a surprise.

RAY. Won't it wait?

EDITH. No. We must have it out now.

RAY *sits. Pause.* EDITH *and* BUCHANAN *exchange glances.*

EDITH. Mr Buchanan is your grandfather. The man who appears with me on my wedding photograph had nothing to do with you. Not even indirectly. I was very silly, and Mr Buchanan behaved badly. We would've got married, only we lost touch with one another. We were too young to know what we were doing. (*Pause.*) Don't blame us too much, Raymond. Try to imagine what it's like to be young.

BUCHANAN. I'm going to marry her. Do the right thing.

RAY *shrugs.*

RAY. Well, understandably I'm shocked by your revelations. The country's moral values far from changing, seem to remain unnaturally constant.

EDITH. I should've told you, I suppose. It would've been easier if your fathers were alive.

RAY *frowns. He turns to* EDITH, *puzzled.*

RAY. My fathers?

EDITH. Yes.

RAY. I had more than one?

> EDITH *clasps her hands in her lap and turns to* BUCHANAN.

EDITH. Just where to stop when telling the truth has always been a problem.

RAY. How could I have two fathers?

EDITH. Your mother was a generous woman. And your fathers – though one of them must surely have been your uncle – loved her dearly. You were the result.

RAY. And my mother?

EDITH. Her pedigree couldn't be subjected to scrutiny either.

> *Silence.* RAY *shakes his head.*

RAY. Bastardy for two generations and on both sides of the family!

BUCHANAN. Had you no idea? No suspicion?

RAY. How could I have?

BUCHANAN. Your birth certificate.

RAY. I've never seen it.

BUCHANAN. When you applied to join in the pension scheme.

RAY. What pension scheme?

BUCHANAN. At your firm. Where you work.

RAY. I don't work.

BUCHANAN. Not work!? (*He stares, open-mouthed.*) What do you do then?

RAY. I enjoy myself.

BUCHANAN. That's a terrible thing to do. I'm bowled over by this, I can tell you. It's my turn to be shocked now. You ought to have a steady job.

EDITH. Two perhaps.

BUCHANAN. In what direction do your talents lie?

RAY. I mended the bathroom tap once.

BUCHANAN. Technically minded, are you?

EDITH. He had nearly thirteen stamps on his card last year. He found himself a lovely situation.

E

RAY. Yes. Only they insisted that I curtail my freedom of speech. These firms make some impossible demands.

BUCHANAN. Is there any particular work you feel you're suited to?

RAY. I took a liftman's job once. For kicks.

BUCHANAN. Kicks? They're very much in the news at the moment, aren't they?

RAY. Yes.

BUCHANAN. Are they doing you any good?

RAY. They're not on prescription, you know.

BUCHANAN. You'll find a good steady job more rewarding in the long run, than purple hearts. I speak from experience. I'm going to talk to Mrs Vealfoy, our personnel lady. She'll advise you what to do with your life.

EDITH (*pause*). Is the toaster ready for trial?

BUCHANAN. Yes.

EDITH. That hand of yours is almost human. The things you contrive to do with it are miraculous.

> BUCHANAN *plugs in the toaster. A loud bang and a flash.*

BUCHANAN. Oh!

> *He cowers away; covers his face with his hands. He begins to shake. Sniffs.*
> *Pause.*

I've never done a thing like that before. I'm quite capable of minor electrical jobs.

> EDITH *leads him to the chair. He sits down. He hunches his shoulders; coughs a little.*

EDITH. You are in a state. We'll have to abandon my original plan of toast for tea.

> RAY *pulls out the plug. He examines the toaster.*

RAY. Where did you get this load of old rubbish?

EDITH. Shhh! (*She nods to* BUCHANAN, *in a quiet voice to* RAY.) It was presented to Mr Buchanan by his firm. As a reward for fifty years' service.

Scene Seven

MRS VEALFOY's *office.*
DEBBIE *enters.* MRS VEALFOY *smiles.*

MRS VEALFOY. Have you any further news, Debbie?
DEBBIE. Yes, Mrs Vealfoy. I saw Raymond last night.
MRS VEALFOY. Did you speak to him?
DEBBIE. I waved, though.
MRS VEALFOY. Did he appear to resent your friendly action?
DEBBIE. No.
MRS VEALFOY. Good. Your relationship with the young man is
   progressing. Were you able to arrange a place of meeting?
DEBBIE. Yes. He sent a message by his friend. He wants to meet
   me at the Skating Rink.
MRS VEALFOY. A skating rink? That doesn't seem advisable in
   your condition, Debbie.
DEBBIE. I thought the same. I said I'd meet him after the Rink
   closed down. Outside.
MRS VEALFOY. And you'll broach the subject of your pregnancy
   whilst he's physically exhausted from an evening's skating?
DEBBIE. Yes.
MRS VEALFOY. Admirable. We're making real headway with the
   problem.
   MRS VEALFOY *pushes several printed forms, typewritten sheets*
   and carbon copies of documents across the desk to DEBBIE.
   Would you read these carefully? I've marked where you're to
   sign.
   DEBBIE *begins to sign the forms.*
   I've made a reservation for a cot at the firm's nurseries. There's
   a query beside the sex of the child. I hope it won't stay that way.
   As DEBBIE *signs the forms she hands them across the desk to*
   MRS VEALFOY.
   A telegram of congratulations will be sent to coincide with the

baby's birth. My secretary has the details of the case. Have no fears. She's most discreet. (*Smiling.*) It won't be long now, my dear, before we place a definite order for your wedding bouquet. As, through no fault of your own, the ceremony looks like being delayed, we'd better make it of some large and showy bloom. Lilies won't be appropriate under the circumstances.

> DEBBIE *pushes the last of the forms across the desk.*

Chrysanthemums would do. Or even peonies.

> *She puts the forms into a wire tray.*

If we leave it much longer it will have to be sunflowers, I'm afraid.

Scene Eight

RAY's *bedroom.*
The room in darkness. The door opens. RAY *enters, guiding* DEBBIE *into the room.*

RAY (*in a whisper*). Don't make a sound.

> *He closes the door carefully and switches on the light.*

(*In a whisper.*) You can open your eyes now.

> DEBBIE *opens her eyes.*

DEBBIE (*looking around, horrified*). What's this?

RAY. Shhh! (*He locks the door.*)

DEBBIE (*in a panic-stricken whisper*). This is a man's bedroom! I can't stay here. It's two o'clock in the morning. What kind of a girl do you take me for?

> *She goes to the door and tries to open it.*

(*Hissing.*) Give me the key!

> *A struggle, both trying not to make any sound.* RAY *almost drags* DEBBIE *to the bed. They sit.*

RAY (*breathes*). You said you'd got something to say to me.

DEBBIE. In your study, you said. This isn't a study. It's a bedroom.

RAY. What's your news?

DEBBIE *stands, shrugs him away.*

DEBBIE (*coldly, after a pause*). I'm having a baby. You're the father. (*She stands by the door.*) Give me the key. I can't be found in a man's bedroom at two in the morning. It's not decent.

Scene Nine

BUCHANAN'*s bedroom, morning.*
On a table, an artificial arm, a pair of glasses, a hearing aid. EDITH *enters.*

EDITH (*drawing the curtains*). Another day! What has it in store? Sunshine or showers?
    She helps BUCHANAN *to sit up and gives him his glasses.*
Now you can see the world.
    She gives him his hearing-aid.
Now you can hear. (*She places several leaflets on the table.*) The post brought some literature for you. I had a quick glance. Nice machines they have, don't they?
    BUCHANAN *picks up a leaflet, glances at it with interest.*
BUCHANAN. They were recently installed.
EDITH. I particularly liked the photos of the canteen. I swept it out once. When one of the kitchen staff was away they sent for me.
BUCHANAN. They recognized your worth?
EDITH. Yes.
BUCHANAN. They're good like that. (*Pause.*) I got these pamphlets for Ray. See if he can't find an interest in life. (*Pause.*) He made a lot of noise last night.
EDITH. These floors are very thin.
BUCHANAN. Sounded like he was dancing.
EDITH. Go and ask him when you've had your breakfast.

Scene Ten

Outside RAY'*s room.*
BUCHANAN *knocks on the door. Pause.*
RAY *opens the door. He is dressed in pyjamas.*

BUCHANAN. I'd like a few words with you, Raymond.
RAY. With me?
BUCHANAN. If it's convenient.
RAY. Just a minute.
He closes the door. Pause. He re-opens it and allows BUCHANAN *into the room.*

Scene Eleven

RAY'*s bedroom.*
BUCHANAN *enters.*

RAY (*with a laugh*). I've just got up. Quite a surprise you gave me.
BUCHANAN. Did I inconvenience you?
RAY. No. I'd just finished.
BUCHANAN. Finished what?
RAY. Well – (*Laughs.*) getting up.
BUCHANAN *sits.*
BUCHANAN. I want a serious talk with you. (*Pause.*) You can't go
on like this, you know.
RAY *doesn't answer.*
Something's missing from your life. Do you know what it is?
RAY *frowns, pause.*
RAY. Is it God?
BUCHANAN (*pause, suspicious*). Who told you about Him?
RAY. I read a bit in the paper once.
BUCHANAN. It's a deep subject, but in my own mind I'm certain
God has nothing to do with you. It's work you want.

BUCHANAN *places several of the firm's pamphlets heavily on the table.*

(*With emphasis.*) My old firm would be delighted to employ you for a small remuneration.

RAY. What about my outside interests?

BUCHANAN. The firm has a Recreation Centre. They cater for most tastes. You'd have to do it after working hours naturally.

RAY. Do what?

BUCHANAN. Whatever you were inclined to. (*Pause.*) Give it a trial.

RAY. I'd like to. Only my plans are in the air at the moment. This bird I've been knocking about with is turning moody. I can't see my way clear to promising anything definite. Either to her or to you. I put something into operation a few months ago which looks like having far-reaching consequences.

Silence.

BUCHANAN. Raymond . . .

RAY. Yes?

BUCHANAN. Is your private life sound?

RAY. As a bell.

BUCHANAN. Good. What would really please your grandmother and me was if you'd find a decent girl and settle down. Do you know any women of the right calibre?

RAY. For what?

BUCHANAN. The altar. You'll have to think about getting married soon.

RAY. That is a distinct possibility.

BUCHANAN. Is she good? This girl you know?

RAY. Blonde with blue eyes. An angelic expression. She has strict views about . . . what we're talking about. I agree with her, of course. Because you should save it up, shouldn't you? Make it go further. Thrift, thrift.

BUCHANAN. Yes. You're not a bad lad at heart, Raymond. (*He indicates the pamphlets.*) Have a glance at these, won't you?

RAY. O.K.

> BUCHANAN *stands. As he does so a coin drops from his pocket and rolls under the bed.*

BUCHANAN. It's under the bed. Can you get it?

RAY. It's only a penny.

BUCHANAN. No, it's half a crown. Move the bed a bit.

RAY. I'll bring it down later.

BUCHANAN. It won't take a minute.

RAY. What's the matter? Think I'm robbing you or something?

> BUCHANAN *stares hard at* RAY. *He glances around the room. Sees* DEBBIE's *handbag on the windowsill. He suddenly bends to look under the bed.*
>
> *Shot of* DEBBIE *crouching under the bed, partly clothed.*
>
> BUCHANAN *straightens up.*

BUCHANAN. You wicked little devil!

> RAY *shrugs.*

This is striking out into new frontiers all right. Eleven o'clock of a Wednesday morning. Women under the bed!

RAY. You should've told me you were coming up.

BUCHANAN. I can hardly credit the degree to which our family has sunk.

RAY. D'you mind going? She's getting covered in dust under there.

> BUCHANAN *goes out.* RAY *lies on the bed.* DEBBIE *emerges.*

DEBBIE. Who was that old man?

RAY. My grandad.

DEBBIE (*opening the wardrobe and taking out her dress*). Why didn't you introduce me properly?

Scene Twelve

The living-room.
BUCHANAN *at the table.* EDITH *brings him a cup of tea and a slice of toast.*

EDITH. What an inconsiderate boy, though, keeping her under the bed. I don't know where he gets his ideas from?

BUCHANAN. I'm outraged by it, I am. Carrying on above our heads. I would never have slept easy if I'd known. Eleven o'clock on a weekday morning! How many of us did that kind of thing?

EDITH. Not many without a priest had sanctioned the act.

BUCHANAN. And not often then.

EDITH. It's something of a miracle we had a succeeding generation we were so unconscious of that side of things.

BUCHANAN. When I met you it was at least in the afternoon.

EDITH. And it was a hot afternoon. Almost evening.

BUCHANAN. I believe it's the lack of proper playing fields.

EDITH. And yet, I'd imagine more open spaces would increase the risk. Does the Duke of Edinburgh realize what he's letting us in for?

RAY enters. Silence. BUCHANAN breaks the silence at last.

BUCHANAN. Well, what have you to say for yourself?

RAY. Let's be fair about it, Grandad. You were upset and so was I. Draw a veil over the whole proceedings.

BUCHANAN. I can't do that.

RAY. Why not?

BUCHANAN. It might happen again.

RAY. Not if you give me warning.

BUCHANAN. We can have it stopped, you know. You're under age. Aren't you? (*Appealing to* EDITH.) Is it legal?

EDITH. He can't vote. I know that.

BUCHANAN. I'm trying to show you a different life from the one you're leading at present. A useful and constructive life such as I've led and –

He begins to cough. EDITH *pats his back.*

Oh, Christ! My lungs'll be on the rug in a minute.

They wait until he recovers.

Who is this girl?

RAY. She lives with her Mum and Dad.

BUCHANAN. What does she do for a living? She doesn't get paid for her activities this morning, does she?

RAY. I wouldn't pay for that.

BUCHANAN. I'm glad you've got a little decency.

RAY. I couldn't afford to.

BUCHANAN. Get a job. You'll have plenty of money then.

RAY. I'd have no time.

BUCHANAN. You'd have the week-ends.

RAY. I'd be too tired.

BUCHANAN. Not if you kept your health.

RAY. How much would I earn?

BUCHANAN. Fifteen pounds a week.

RAY. Where does fifteen quid go with a woman?

BUCHANAN. If you're determined to persevere with women I can see no future for you. There are other group activities, you know.

RAY. Yes, but the rules are in French.

BUCHANAN. Learn the language. Acquire a fluency in something else. Ludo would be less of a strain in the long run.

    DEBBIE *enters. She stands uneasily at the door. Her lip trembles.*

DEBBIE. I'm sorry to barge in on you, but I'll have to be going. I'm late for work.

RAY (*pause, embarrassed*). This is Miss Fieldman. Debbie – my grandfather and grandmother.

    Silence. DEBBIE *shuffles her feet, ill at ease.*

BUCHANAN. What explanation have you got for being under a man's bed at this time in the day?

DEBBIE. I'm sorry. It must seem awful to you. I had important news to communicate to Ray last night. And he persuaded me to stay.

EDITH. Were you under the bed all night?

DEBBIE. No. (*Pause, she becomes tearful.*) I'm not really like that at all. (*Crying.*) I'm having a baby! (*Defiant.*) I'm seeing someone this morning from the Welfare. (*To* RAY.) You'll have to settle it with them. They'll want details. I can't manage on my own.

BUCHANAN (*shocked, to* EDITH). He's put her in the family way. That is an act of indecency I will not tolerate. He must go.

EDITH. It's the sex-education. They think of nothing else.

RAY. We didn't receive any sex-education.

BUCHANAN. How did you learn?

RAY. From other boys.

BUCHANAN. What kind of boys are these that teach each other about the family way? Get away from me, Raymond. I'm disappointed in you.

RAY. But you did the same.

BUCHANAN. I had every excuse. Conditions were bad. You want for nothing today.

DEBBIE dries her eyes.

DEBBIE (*to* RAY). I can't stay any longer. I'm late as it is. (*She dabs at her nose.*) My Mum and Dad want to meet you. They don't know what's happened. Mum's arranging an outing next week and I thought that'd be a good opportunity of telling them.

She takes his arm.

See me to the door.

RAY and DEBBIE go out. BUCHANAN picks up a piece of toast. He puts it down in disgust.

BUCHANAN (*wearily*). Something's wrong with this toast.

EDITH. It's your toaster. It carries on in a most eccentric fashion. And the clock is about as useful. Tells whatever time it fancies.

BUCHANAN goes to the shelf and picks up the clock.

BUCHANAN. It's going backwards! Something's wrong with the works. (*He turns the clock over and drops it.*) Oh!

EDITH. What is it?

BUCHANAN. Gave me a shock it did. Right up my arm.

He puts the clock beside the toaster on the table.

EDITH (*with a shrug*). They seem more like murder weapons than gifts from a grateful employer.

Scene Thirteen

MRS VEALFOY'*s office.*

MRS VEALFOY *speaking to a recording machine.*

MRS VEALFOY. Anyone found using the staff lifts without permission will be liable to instant dismissal. (*Pause.*) Circulate copies to all departments.

Silence.

Another notice. To all heads of departments. Capitals. LONELY PEOPLE. (*Pause.*) If you know of anyone who would be interested in joining the firm's recently formed 'Bright Hours' club would you kindly contact Mrs Vealfoy or any member of her staff. The person or persons of either sex must be old, lonely and ex-members of the firm. No other qualifications are needed.

She speaks on the intercom to her secretary.

Send Miss Fieldman in.

She turns to the mirror, and puts on her hat. DEBBIE *enters.*

MRS VEALFOY. Have you seen the young man?

DEBBIE. Yes, Mrs Vealfoy.

MRS VEALFOY. Have you told him the facts of the case?

DEBBIE. Yes.

MRS VEALFOY. Has he given you his address?

DEBBIE. Yes.

She takes a postcard from her handbag, and gives it to MRS VEALFOY.

MRS VEALFOY (*taking the postcard*). You may go. I'll contact your Supervisor immediately I've any news.

DEBBIE *goes out.* MRS VEALFOY *speaks to her secretary over the intercom.*

I'll be away for about an hour.

Scene Fourteen

EDITH's *living-room*.
EDITH *enters followed by* MRS VEALFOY.

MRS VEALFOY. Are you sure your grandson isn't at home?

EDITH. Yes. He's away for the day.

MRS VEALFOY. Is he seeking employment?

EDITH. I couldn't say. We've grown apart lately. We hardly exchange two words together.

MRS VEALFOY. Why?

EDITH. I didn't like to ask. They're so touchy these days.

    MRS VEALFOY *takes out a card.*

MRS VEALFOY. See that he gets this. I want to see him. Tell him that. Tell him that Mrs Vealfoy is anxious to have a word with him.

    EDITH *puts the card on the shelf.*

  Is Mr Buchanan in?

EDITH. Well, he's in. Whether I consider he's in a fit state to receive visitors is a different matter.

MRS VEALFOY (*with a smile*). We must do something about that.

EDITH. He's been upset.

MRS VEALFOY. Has he had a check-up? Give me the name of his medical practitioner.

EDITH. He's depressed.

MRS VEALFOY. Is that the truth? I think I can clear things up.

EDITH. He broods, see.

MRS VEALFOY. Question him why he does that. Worm it out of him.

EDITH. Our grandson has misbehaved himself. The clock and the toaster have proved a disappointment. And to cap it all he's old. So what with one thing and another his attitude is of despair.

MRS VEALFOY (*sharply*). What did you say?

EDITH. He despairs.

MRS VEALFOY. Has he used that word in your presence?

EDITH. No.

MRS VEALFOY. He should forget about it. And to take his mind off things why not busy himself? A part-time job. Join a club. Make himself so busy he hasn't time to despair.

EDITH. He'll exhaust himself, poor darling.

MRS VEALFOY. What hobbies has he?

EDITH. None, if you can believe him. And personally I do. We have that sort of relationship, see?

MRS VEALFOY. Where is he now?

EDITH. In bed.

MRS VEALFOY (*laughing*). In bed? That isn't doing him any good, is it? He must take this matter seriously.

EDITH. We're going to be married on Saturday.

MRS VEALFOY. Are you? That's a good idea. Are you having a cake?

EDITH. No. We're not having anything. It's only for show. It's a waste getting married when you're my age. I'm only doing it for his sake. He's very much on his dignity about it. He's been like that all his life so he tells me. I can't vouch for it, of course, as I only met him briefly at the beginning and at the end.

MRS VEALFOY. Mr Buchanan must come to the 'Bright Hours' club. He'll meet old friends. I'll expect him. (*She opens her handbag, and takes out a circular.*) See that he's there. He'll forget his troubles, you'll see.

Scene Fifteen

MRS VEALFOY's *office*.

MRS VEALFOY *at her desk.* RAY *enters.* MRS VEALFOY *indicates a chair.*

MRS VEALFOY. Come along in, Raymond. Sit down.

RAY *sits,* MRS VEALFOY *smiles.*

MRS VEALFOY. I can't tell you how glad I am to meet you. I'm taking a great interest in you at the moment. (*Laughs.*) I hope that doesn't alarm you?

RAY. No.

MRS VEALFOY. Good. (*Laughs.*) Good. You know, Raymond, we're all pretty worried about you. How do you feel? Are you worried?

RAY. Yes.

MRS VEALFOY. I'm glad to hear it. There's nothing so impressive as disquiet in the young. It shows an awareness of the problems of life which is most encouraging.

She studies RAY *for a moment with a quizzical expression.*

One of the things that has caused me great concern is the apparent lack of any real direction to your life. And I think that this has caused your trouble. Don't you?

RAY (*not wishing to disagree*). Yes.

MRS VEALFOY. Ah, I'm glad you used that particular word. An affirmation of anything is cheering nowadays. Say 'Yes' as often as possible, Raymond. I always do. (*Laughs.*) Always. (*Smiles.*) Now, you must count me as a friend. A friend who will do all in her power to help you. Do you understand me?

RAY. Yes.

MRS VEALFOY. That's the spirit. (*Laughs.*) My goodness, we are getting on well, aren't we? (*She laughs and then, suddenly, serious.*) Do you love Debbie?

RAY. Yes.

MRS VEALFOY. And do you agree that what you have done is wrong?

RAY *attempts to speak.* MRS VEALFOY *holds up her hand, smiles.*

I'm not passing judgement. I merely want to ask if you agree with me. Do you think it wrong? (*Smiles.*) You don't have to say 'Yes' if you disagree with me. (*Pause.*) Do you think what you've done is wrong?

RAY. No.

MRS VEALFOY. I see. (*She smiles with no trace of disapproval.*) And why don't you think it is wrong?

RAY. If two people love each other why shouldn't they make love?

MRS VEALFOY (*simply and with candour*). Raymond, you mustn't imagine for one moment that I'm against two people expressing their love for each other. I'm most certainly not. Love-making is a beautiful thing. And we must treat it with the respect it deserves. Physical love is one of the finest ways a man can express his feelings for a woman. Therefore he must be very sure indeed that he really loves the woman to whom he gives his love. (*Pause.*) Do you really love Debbie?

RAY. Yes.

MRS VEALFOY. You want her to be happy?

RAY. I'm going to marry her.

MRS VEALFOY. That isn't quite the same thing. A baby on the way is no excuse for marriage nowadays. No one would suggest it was.

RAY. I want to marry her.

MRS VEALFOY. Good. (*Smiles.*) I always like the end achieved to coincide with established practice, though the means to the end may vary with custom. (*Pause.*) You see, Raymond, I think what you have done *is* wrong. Not for any religious reason (I'm an agnostic myself), but simply because love-making should be kept for one's marriage partner alone. Outside marriage the act may seem the same, but I have my doubts as to whether anyone derives any real and lasting satisfaction from it. There is no finer sight than two married people making love.

She looks at RAY *seriously.*

This thoughtless and selfish act may lead you to a much more worthwhile view of life. (*Pause.*) When you're married and have a wife and child you'll have to accept responsibility for them.

RAY. Yes.

MRS VEALFOY. You'll want a regular wage packet each week. (*With a smile, coup de grâce.*) And so, you see, you must have a steady job. It's high time you began to consider a career.

She takes a form from her desk and pushes it across to RAY.
Just fill that in, Raymond. (*Laughs.*) And afterwards I'll take
you down to our various departments. Show you round. See
what vacancies we have.

Scene Sixteen

A room in the firm's recreation centre.
*A number of old ex-employees are grouped around an upright piano
singing: 'We'll All Go Riding on a Rainbow to a New Land Far
Away'. Weary, apathetic voices.*
MRS VEALFOY *enters with* BUCHANAN. *She takes him to the group.*

MRS VEALFOY. Stop one moment everybody. (*The music dies
away.*) This is George. Do any of us remember him? (*Pause.*)
George retired recently after – how long, George?

BUCHANAN. Fifty years.

MRS VEALFOY. Fifty years. Yes, I believe I remember you. We
gave you an electric clock. Is that correct?

BUCHANAN. Yes.

MRS VEALFOY. And an electric shaver —

BUCHANAN. Toaster.

MRS VEALFOY. Toaster. Does anybody remember George?
Everybody stares at BUCHANAN. *No one says anything.*
Nobody? Are we sure? He has a distinctive face. Are we quite
sure we none of us are acquainted with our new member?
An OLD MAN *puts up his hand.*

OLD MAN. I remember him.

MRS VEALFOY *smiles.*

MRS VEALFOY. Isn't that nice. An old workmate of yours,
George. So you won't feel out of it.
The group around the piano drift away. MRS VEALFOY *takes*
BUCHANAN *around the room.*
Over here we have dominoes, cards and darts and all the pas-
times.

F

She points out a group of OLD MEN *and* WOMEN. *Two of them are in wheelchairs, one is blind, a couple are simple-minded. They stare at* BUCHANAN *without interest.* MRS VEALFOY *smiles and takes* BUCHANAN *across the room.*

And over here we have conversation.

Two or three VERY OLD WOMEN *are knitting.*

Would you like to talk over old times?

BUCHANAN. Yes.

MRS VEALFOY. Tea at three o'clock. Go and talk to your friend.

BUCHANAN goes over to the OLD MAN.

BUCHANAN. Hallo.

OLD MAN. Hallo, George.

BUCHANAN. I've never been in this room before.

OLD MAN. It's private.

BUCHANAN says nothing. A WOMAN *at the end of the room falls over. A flutter of excitement.* MRS VEALFOY *hurries to help her up. It is seen distantly.*

BUCHANAN. You remember me then?

OLD MAN. I retired a bit before you.

BUCHANAN. Did you see my photo in the magazine?

OLD MAN. No.

BUCHANAN. I was a long-service employee. A credit to canteen food they said I was. (*Pause.*) That's their words. I had dinner there since it opened. Can't be much wrong with the food, can there?

OLD MAN. I never used the canteen. I never liked that big woman as ran it.

BUCHANAN. She lost her husband recently.

OLD MAN. Is she left then?

Two OLD MEN *in wheelchairs pass across the room in the distance. A group has formed about the woman who fell over.* MRS VEALFOY *at the centre.*

Who was her husband? Did he work for us?

BUCHANAN. He was on the maintenance staff.

OLD MAN. I'm not up in that side of the firm. It never interested me.

MRS VEALFOY is seen shooing people away from the fallen woman. Two stretcher bearers have entered the room. The woman is put on the stretcher and hurried away. MRS VEALFOY's voice is heard faintly, from the distance.

MRS VEALFOY. Go back to what you were doing. It's quite all right. Off you go.

The group breaks up, wanders away.

OLD MAN. She's dead.

BUCHANAN. Who?

OLD MAN. The old girl as fell over. Didn't you see her?

BUCHANAN. No.

OLD MAN. Yes. She'll be dead.

Silence.

BUCHANAN. I looked forward to my retirement so's I could play skittles full time. I used to be a fan. I was in line for the cup. I just missed it. The mysterious thing was that I never came in line for it again.

OLD MAN. Bowls is my sport.

BUCHANAN. That's a nice game.

OLD MAN. I was almost mentioned in a well-known sporting periodical once.

BUCHANAN. I never got as far as that.

OLD MAN. I regard that as the high-spot of my life.

BUCHANAN. Yes. You would. (*Pause.*) The high-spot of my own career came when my photo appeared in the magazine. I didn't ask them to put it in. Some of them go round canvassing for support in their claims to be included. But I stood aside. And one day they came to my department and insisted I pose for them. I was unwilling at first. But I realized it was for my own good.

Silence.

MRS VEALFOY. Just one moment everybody. Listen to me please. Are you attending to what I say? (*Pause.*) Good.

She holds up a painting.

Isn't this delightful? Do you know who painted it?

OLD MAN (*calling*). You, miss!

Laughter.

MRS VEALFOY (*laughing*). What a flattering suggestion. No, I'm sure you didn't really think I could have done such a charming work of art. (*Pause.*) Well, since you pretend you can't tell me – Mrs Florence Thompson painted this splendid example of creative activity. Isn't she talented? Forty years on the shop floor hasn't dimmed her appreciation of the beautiful. Let's show our delight by a round of applause. Come along.

A patter of applause.

(*Putting the picture down.*) Everybody get on with what they were doing.

OLD MAN (*to* BUCHANAN). Where did you work?

BUCHANAN. I was almost Staff.

OLD MAN (*impressed*). Were you?

BUCHANAN. I was in charge of the Main Entrance. I saw the Chairman of the Board several times. I've even opened the door to him once. My immediate Superior was off with 'flu.

OLD MAN. You were on the doors?

BUCHANAN. It's a type of service I approve of.

Silence.

The local press sent somebody round last week.

OLD MAN. We don't take the local press.

BUCHANAN. You're like us then. Like us. I spoke a few words about my thoughts. I'm against the local paper because of the things they say about the Memorial to the Fallen. 'Isn't it a disgusting eyesore' and all that.

Silence. BUCHANAN *stares blankly ahead.*

(*At last.*) Who are these people who have no respect for the dead of two world wars? I'm bitter about it, I am. We fought for that Memorial. Men died for it.

OLD MAN. What edition were you in?

BUCHANAN. Ah, they didn't print it. Too controversial, I expect.
  MRS VEALFOY *comes over.*

MRS VEALFOY. What are you saying? Is it interesting? Can I
  hear? Are you talking over old times as I told you?

BUCHANAN. No.

MRS VEALFOY. Why not? What were you talking about? Both of
  you have a lot to look back on. (*Pause, sharply.*) Answer my
  question! What were you talking about?

BUCHANAN. The war.

MRS VEALFOY. Were you in the war? (*Laughs.*)

BUCHANAN. I helped out as best I could. Three nights a week I
  was required to firewatch.

MRS VEALFOY. Who required you to do that?

BUCHANAN. Why – (*Puzzled.*) we all did it.

MRS VEALFOY. Good for you! Did you enjoy yourself? Were you
  on the roof?

BUCHANAN. Yes.

MRS VEALFOY. Splendid! I'm going to tell that to my friends.
  You see, I'll draw you out. You don't talk enough. (*Laughs.*)
  What happened before the war?

BUCHANAN. I can't recollect.

MRS VEALFOY. What a short memory you have. (*Laughs.*) Still,
  you've had a very full life without a long memory, haven't you?
  You must tell me sometime how you managed. (*Pause, she
  smiles at him, benevolently.*) And after the war? What did you do
  after the war?

  BUCHANAN *is silent.*

  Like that is it? You don't wish to talk? Keeping the fascinating
  details to yourself. (*Laughs.*) Well, you must tell me some day.
  Is that a promise?

BUCHANAN. Yes.

MRS VEALFOY. Good for you. Are you getting on well with your
  friend? Is he showing you the ropes? Are you having a good
  time?

BUCHANAN (*without conviction*). Yes.

MRS VEALFOY. That's the main thing. What about your depression? Have you forgotten about it?

BUCHANAN. No.

MRS VEALFOY. Why not?

BUCHANAN. I can't forget it. (*Pause.*) You wouldn't understand.

MRS VEALFOY (*laughs*). Don't say that to me. I understand everything. (*Laughs.*) Bring your problems to me. I'll unravel any difficulties. So don't let me catch you being depressed. (*Pause.*) Were you in the war? Is that why you're depressed? Did you have a terrible time? (*Pause.*) What did you do?

BUCHANAN. I was required to firewatch.

MRS VEALFOY. Who required you to do that? (*Pause.*) You don't like talking about it. Such a terrible time. (*Laughs brightly.*) We're going to sing in a minute. That will cure your depression, won't it? Will you join in? A jolly sing-song. All the old favourites. Don't be a spoil-sport. You'll join in, won't you?

BUCHANAN. Is it hymns?

MRS VEALFOY (*suddenly her face becomes set and serious*). We're strictly non-denominational. We can't have hymns. I'm sorry, but you know how it is.

She goes to the centre of the room.

Stop whatever you're doing! (*Pause.*) Now, before the sing-song, who is coming to the annual get-together? All of you, I'm sure. I want to make sure you all have tickets. Two tickets for each former employee. Only one visitor is allowed. (*Laughs.*) Come along now!

The ex-employees move towards MRS VEALFOY, *she hands out the tickets.*

OLD MAN (*to* BUCHANAN, *with curiosity*). Is your name Hyams?

BUCHANAN. No.

OLD MAN. Isn't it? (*Pause.*) Surely you're Georgie Hyams?

BUCHANAN. No, that's never been my name. My name is Buchanan.

OLD MAN (*getting up from his seat*). I'm afraid I don't know you then.

BUCHANAN. But – (*Shocked.*) you said you did.

OLD MAN (*moving towards the group around* MRS VEALFOY). I made a mistake. I thought you were an old mate of mine. His name was Hyams.

BUCHANAN (*catching hold of the* OLD MAN'*s sleeve*). You don't know me then?

OLD MAN. No.

BUCHANAN. But I worked here. I was on the main entrance. Are you sure you don't remember me?

OLD MAN. I'm sorry.

> *He shrugs* BUCHANAN *off and moves to the group around* MRS VEALFOY.

BUCHANAN. Nobody knows me. They've never seen me before.

> MRS VEALFOY *claps her hands together.*

MRS VEALFOY. We're going to run through all the songs with 'Happy' in them. Let's bang out the words. Never mind the tune. We'll muddle through somehow.

> *The pianist strikes up 'Here We Are Again, Happy As Can Be'. The ex-employees crowd round the piano.* MRS VEALFOY *in the centre.* BUCHANAN'*s face is glimpsed. He begins to sing. Stops. Sings again. Several old, tired and depressed faces are seen.* MRS VEALFOY'*s laughing face is seen as the music abruptly changes to 'Happy Days Are Here Again'.* BUCHANAN *stops singing and moves away from the group.* MRS VEALFOY *is beside him instantly.*

MRS VEALFOY (*raising her voice slightly above the singing*). Why aren't you joining in?

BUCHANAN. I don't know the words.

MRS VEALFOY. Follow me then. Repeat everything I say. Is that clear? What were you thinking just now?

BUCHANAN. Nothing.

MRS VEALFOY. I don't allow thoughts like that. So come on, cheer up, and if you don't know the words just hum the tune.

> *She leads him back to the centre of the group, between two old men in wheelchairs.* BUCHANAN *joins in the singing.*

(*Her voice soaring above the rest as the music changes.*)
'I want to be Happy,
But I can't be Happy,
Till I've made you Happy too'.

Scene Seventeen

EDITH's *living-room.*
BUCHANAN *stands beside the table. On the table the clock and the*
     toaster. He lifts a hammer and smashes them to pieces.

Scene Eighteen

BUCHANAN's *bedroom.*
BUCHANAN *in bed.* EDITH *enters.*

EDITH. Another day has dawned. Bright and clear. Let's be thankful for it.
     She plumps BUCHANAN's *pillow, hands him his glasses and*
     hearing-aid.
Look at the sun streaming through the window. A few weeks
ago you'd have been at work. Now you can enjoy the good
weather when it comes and you fall sick. That's no way to carry
on.
     She smiles at him.
The photos are here!
     She shows him a series of wedding photographs. They show, in
     succession: DEBBIE *arriving at the church,* DEBBIE *and* RAY
     at the altar, DEBBIE *and* RAY *signing the register after the*
     ceremony, DEBBIE *and* RAY *walking down the aisle of the*
     church, DEBBIE *and* RAY *in front of the church doors.*
     As the photographs are shown, the opening bars of Mendelssohn's
     wedding march are heard. This is abruptly cut off as the sixth
     photograph is shown – DEBBIE *fainting among a group of*
     bridesmaids – and a wailing cry of a newborn child is heard.

Her dress was quite ruined.

She puts the photographs to one side.

Aren't you interested, dear? (*Pause.*) The holiday season will soon be upon us. Everybody is talking of nothing else. There's a twitter in the air. A woman at work is taking her car abroad this year. She's on top of the world thinking about it. She's a dedicated holiday maker.

BUCHANAN *lies back, stares at the ceiling.*

Why, you're crying. (*She kisses him.*) Tears running down your cheeks. (*She hugs him.*) The tickets have arrived for the 'get-together'. It's to be held at the Bell Hotel. They've hired a name band. It's to be gayer than ever this year. So much laughter, so much joy in people's hearts, so many happy faces all around. Raymond will qualify for a ticket. So will Debbie. And Debbie's parents are going because they qualify. So we shall be a big party. I'm buying a new dress for the occasion. And I shall smile a lot, more than usual, because we have so much to be thankful for.

BUCHANAN *closes his eyes and dies.*

Raymond has quite reformed. Sees the error of his ways now. That's Debbie's influence. So you see even doing wrong as he did has its uses.

A clipping from a newspaper's 'Births, Marriages and Deaths' column is seen.

'DEATHS: At his home in Swinton Street, George Buchanan. Sadly missed by his wife, Edith, grandson, Raymond, and workmates. No flowers by request.'

EDITH (*continuing the previous speech over the newspaper clipping*). It got him married. Settled. With a future before him.

Scene Nineteen

The Bell Hotel.
Dance band playing. Dancers. Music comes to an end. MRS VEAL-FOY *steps on to the platform. Speaks into microphone.*

MRS VEALFOY. In the next dance the Gentlemen employees are
at liberty to ask the Directors' wives for a dance. And I think
we can invent a new little rule here – just a tiny new rule – the
Lady Employees can ask the Directors for a dance. (*Laughter.*)
Now, don't be shy. They're just the same as you are.

The band begins to play softly.

Before we carry on with our fun I have to announce a sad
death. George Buchanan passed away last week. His wife
wishes me to express thanks to all in the firm who sent beautiful
floral tributes in her sad bereavement. And now, on with the
dance and let us pray for good weather during the holiday
season.

*The band plays 'On the Sunny Side of the Street'. Dancers fill
the floor. At the side of the dance-floor, EDITH is seen with
DEBBIE's family. The non-dancing employees begin to sing the
words of the song. Everybody is singing, MRS VEALFOY is seen
in company with the board of directors, they also are singing.*

Methuen's Modern Plays

EDITED BY JOHN CULLEN

Methuen Playscripts

Johnny Speight	*If There Weren't Any Blacks You'd Have To Invent Them*
Martin Sperr	*Tales From Landshut*
Boris Vian	*The Knacker's ABC*
Lanford Wilson	*Home Free! and The Madness of Lady Bright*

★   ★   ★

Methuen's Theatre Classics

DANTON'S DEATH	Buechner
	an English version by James Maxwell
THE TROJAN WOMEN	Euripides
	an English version by Neil Curry
IRONHAND	Goethe
	adapted by John Arden
THE GOVERNMENT INSPECTOR	Gogol
	an English version by Edward O. Marsh and Jeremy Brooks
THE REDEMPTION	*adapted by Gordon Honeycombe from five cycles of Mystery Plays*
LADY PRECIOUS STREAM	*adapted by S. I. Hsiung from a sequence of traditional Chinese plays*
BRAND	Ibsen
HEDDA GABLER	*translated by Michael Meyer*
THE WILD DUCK	
THE MASTER BUILDER	